The New Testament in the Life of the Church

The New Testament in the Life of the Church

Evangelization Prayer
Catechetics Homiletics

by Eugene LaVerdiere s.s.s.

AVE MARIA PRESS
Notre Dame, Indiana 46556

© 1980 Ave Maria Press, Notre Dame, Indiana 46556

International Standard Book Number: 0-87793-213-1

Library of Congress Catalog Card Number: 80-67403

Printed and bound in the United States

Cover design by Joyce Stanley DePalma

*To my brothers
in the Congregation of the Most Blessed Sacrament*

Eugene LaVerdiere, a member of the Blessed Sacrament Fathers, brings an impressive background in biblical scholarship to his writing. He has attended and earned degrees from John Carroll University in Cleveland, the University of Fribourg in Switzerland, the Pontifical Biblical Institute in Rome, the Ecole Biblique in Jerusalem, and the University of Chicago.

Father LaVerdiere speaks widely at conferences and workshops around the world and has written numerous magazine and journal articles. He is the author of several books, including *Trumpets of Beaten Metal* (Liturgical Press), *Invitation to New Testament Epistles II* (Doubleday) and *Luke* (Glazier). Father LaVerdiere currently teaches at the Chicago Theological Union.

Contents

Introduction

The New Testament in the Life of the Church

The life of the church is a life of shared faith, vibrant love and firm hope. Experienced in community and nourished by centuries of tradition, this life looks courageously to a long future whose contours are as yet undisclosed and which will surely be full of surprises.

Within this history, the church has a role to play, a multifaceted role in which it extends the life-giving and liberating presence of Christ to a needy world. Such is the church's primary mission of evangelization. To exercise it fruitfully, the church's own inner life must be healthy and mature. For this purpose, it exercises a ministry of catechesis in which it nourishes its own members with Christian understanding and wisdom.

Born of God, the church's life must be ever attuned to God. The church thus assembles to hear God's word and to speak its own word to him in a liturgy which propels it into the Christian mission. This essential life function is assured by the Liturgy of the Word, with its readings, meditations, professions of faith, acclamations, prayers and homily. The quality of the liturgy, however, depends on the personal lives of those who gather for its celebration. Like the church, which gathers for the liturgy, individual Christians must also be attuned to God. The main source and the barometer of their attunement is personal prayer.

In its life, and more specifically in the ministries of the word and in prayer, the church communicates and expresses the word of God which became incarnate in Christ. To do this, it turns to the scriptures and especially to the New Testament, whose divine and human word is a classical statement of what it means to be Christian. For the New Testament's message to be plain and relevant, however, it must be interpreted.

This book is about the interpretation of the New Testament in the life of the church. More specifically, it is about New Testament interpretation in the church's mission of *evangelization* and *catechesis,* in liturgical preaching or *homiletics* and in *prayer.*

Interpretation

This book is about interpretation, not however about the methods of interpretation which have been developed and refined in modern times. For the most part, these methods respond to our need for understanding and they supply carefully honed processes which yield a good and accurate understanding of texts. My interest is rather in methods of interpretation for communication and expression, and for this purpose the various methods of interpretation for understanding are not adequate. This becomes clear from a brief review of these methods with special emphasis on the questions to which they respond.

1) There are the various forms of *literary criticism.* Decades ago, this type of interpretation focused on the meaning of language and its special usage by a given author. Today, its concern is mainly with the broader modes of literary communication, and it focuses on form, structure, movement and special matters such as irony and hyperbole.

2) There is *form criticism*, which isolates and describes the pre-literary elements which were assumed into our literary texts. These elements include hymns, creeds, acclamations, stories, liturgical formulas, homilies and catechetical materials, all of which had their natural setting in the church's oral communication before finding literary expression in the books of the New Testament.

3) There is *redaction criticism*, which compares literary texts with one another and with the oral forms isolated through form criticism. Its purpose is to uncover each author's intention, and its main concern is to clarify a particular author's unique theological contribution to New Testament literature.

4) There is *historical criticism*, a difficult effort which uses all the techniques of historical research as these have developed in modern times. Its aim is to isolate and describe the events which lie behind the literary expression, the oral forms and the theological reflection which contributed to the making of the New Testament. Its purpose is to provide a basis for evaluating and understanding these later developments.

5) There is what is now called *hermeneutics.* The four previous methods led to an understanding of the text in its New Testament context, and they can be grouped under the general term "exegesis." Hermeneutics, on the other hand, seeks to understand the New Testament text in its present-day context. Its concern is not with what the text once said to people but with what and how the same text addresses people living in a vastly changed context.

All five of these methods of interpretation have become indispensable for a full understanding of the

New Testament. But suppose our questions are not with the author's use of language and literary forms of expression, with the spoken forms which he assumed into his work, with his theological reflection and its literary articulation, with the events which underlie all of these or with how the text now addresses us. Suppose our questions do not have to do with understanding but with our active use and communication of these texts in evangelization, catechesis, homiletics and prayer. What then? Do we not need a new form or several new forms of interpretation which correspond to an entirely different set of questions?

This book is about forms of interpretation for communication and expression rather than for understanding. Such interpretation corresponds to the active pastoral or apostolic stance of one who engages in the life of the church and not to the quasi-passive stance of one who reads the New Testament merely to know what it says. This is not to deny that interpretation for understanding is useful or to claim that it is outdated, but to affirm that it is not fully adequate to the needs of church life and ministry. For example, once we have studied and understood a text, a whole new type of reflection is needed to communicate it in a homily or in catechesis. These ministerial functions are based on study, but they are seriously deformed when they are replaced by an exegetical or hermeneutical lecture.

Obviously, understanding will result from communication and expression. However, the communicator's primary purpose is not to achieve understanding for himself or herself. Rather, the communicator is like one who finds life and salvation, not by seeking these but by offering them to others.

Introduction

The New Testament

This book is about the interpretation of the New Testament. It deals with the interpretation of its various books, 27 in all, some long, some short, some intimately related to others by reason of a common source, identity of authorship, a like purpose, the same addressees, or a similar social situation. However, it also deals with the collection as a whole, our New Testament, which the church recognizes as distinct from the Old Testament and as a complex unit from which Christians draw life and guidance in their mission.

Actually, the book could have dealt with the Old Testament as well, since the Old Testament is joined to the New as an integral part of the church's Bible. So viewed, the Old Testament finds its living context in the church, and it is from the point of view of the church that it is interpreted by Christians. Such a context differs from that of Judaism, which also recognizes the Old Testament as its sacred book and word of God. For Jews, this unique point of reference is indicated in the rejection of the term, "Old Testament," a designation which presupposes the existence and acceptance of the New Testament. In Judaism, our Old Testament is called the scriptures, the Hebrew Bible or the Tanak, an acronym for the *Torah* or Law (T), the *Nebiim* or prophets (N) and the *Ketubim* or Writings (K).

The various methods of interpretation which will be presented can easily be applied to the Old Testament. This book does not do so for three reasons.

1) My principal area of biblical study is the New Testament, and it appeared simpler to draw the many examples which are needed from that limited source.

2) The New Testament was actually born in the

15

church to which we also belong. It was thus possible to study the New Testament from the point of view of its function in the ministerial and prayer life of the early church. Since the early church and the New Testament did use the Old Testament a great deal, the latter will not be altogether excluded. However, it will be approached from its New Testament usage and vantage point.

3) By limiting the book's scope to the New Testament, it was possible to achieve greater focus. The interpretation of a text is conditioned by the particular ministerial task in which we are engaged. As we refer to many of the same texts in relation to different pastoral functions, we should discover more of the potential which these texts hold, and the distinction between the methods of interpretation should become clearer.

The Life of the Church

This book is about the interpretation of the New Testament in the life of the church. The New Testament outlived its authors and original addressees and was appropriated by the church as its extremely special book, a classical expression of the word of God. Times have changed over and over again, and so have the church's internal and external challenges. However, the living, believing community of the church, which stands in continuity with its New Testament origins, has always been the context *par excellence* for interpreting the scriptures. I say *par excellence* because the church represents the very context in which the New Testament scriptures were born. It thus constitutes their natural habitat or home. From the point of view of the impulse which created them, every other context is consequently artificial, at least in part. This applies to every secular realm, including the secular university and classroom. These may shed much light on the New Testament, but it is not the light of faith in quest of understanding or Christian expression and communication.

The above position concerning the church as the primary context of interpretation applies to the various methods of interpretation for understanding. *A fortiori*, it applies to methods of expressive and communicative interpretation.

The methods of communicative interpretation correspond to the church's many apostolic and pastoral functions. These include *evangelization*, an apostolic mission in which the church reaches out to those who have not heard the Gospel of God concerning his Son, a Gospel which remains a living word in the church community. They also include *catechesis*, a pastoral mission in which the church enlightens those who have been evangelized in order that they might live as responsible adult Christians. Evangelization flows into catechesis, and catechesis flows out of evangelization. Formally, however, these apostolic and pastoral functions are distinct and call for different attitudes and methods of interpretation.

In addition, there is *homiletics*, a pastoral function intimately related to the church's liturgical life, and especially to the celebration of the Eucharist. Method in homiletics springs from a good sense of what the Eucharist is about, how it is related to people's lives and how they interrelate in the celebration. It presupposes that a people has been evangelized and catechized to a certain extent and that they have heard the biblical word in the sacramental act of Eucharist.

Prayer is yet another major function of the church, a function in which Christians individually and communally turn to God. Unlike the three previous functions, its focus is not so much on communication as on listening and expression. With this distinction, I mean to disassociate prayer from communication with other human beings, which is a ready danger in shared prayer. Prayer is indeed a form of communication, but communication with God is vastly different from communication within the human community.

The four functions which I have described are the subject of the four main chapters of the book. They are not meant as an exhaustive list. Further work would need to be done on areas such as the use of the New Testament in the sacrament of reconciliation, in spiritual direction and in theological reflection. These and other areas have been set aside for the future. The response of colleagues in biblical studies and in the pastoral field to the present limited effort will contribute to their elaboration.

Each of the four chapters includes an introduction, in which the apostolic or pastoral area is briefly presented and related to major statements of the church in recent times. There follows a section on the witness of the New Testament concerning both the area being considered and interpretation or method in that area. Third, each chapter contains a development on appropriate methods for using the New Testament scriptures in the respective ministerial areas. Fourth and finally, each chapter includes a long bibliographical note, in which I take up various resources which have been helpful to me, which provide a good example or presentation of some of the issues treated, or in which I myself have developed a particular question. In this note, I shall present matters which would normally have appeared in footnotes. This approach was used to assure greater readability and usefulness.

The various methods of interpretation are not viewed as exclusive. Others engaged in the biblical apostolate have developed good methods for using the New Testament. Those which I present have been developed in the field, while working with numerous persons and organizations at the parish, diocesan and national levels in the United States and in several other countries, including some in the Third World. It would be futile to try to name them all. Those who have participated in this work and who have urged me to write on the subject will recognize their contribution. From the very nature of the task, their contribution was indispensable.

Bibliographical Note

We cannot ignore a frequent question addressed to biblical scholars, whose prodigious work is constantly discovering additional meaning in New Testament texts. How is it possible that we can know so much about the New Testament when previous generations or even centuries of church history knew so little? Are we not being pretentious? This does not seem consonant with the Lord's guiding presence in the church. More specifically, how is it possible that the Fathers of the church, who lived much closer to New Testament times, failed to understand or missed the point when we can find the meaning? Must we conclude that the church in modern times knows more than the Fathers knew?

In its various forms, the question is a valid one, and

one with which many have struggled. The distinction we have made between interpretation for understanding and interpretation for communication and expression suggests an answer. The Fathers of the church, men like Tertullian, Ambrose, Augustine, John Chrysostom and Cyril of Jerusalem, were not engaged in a pure search for understanding the New Testament but in communicating its message in the apostolic and pastoral life of the church. Their concern was with the use of the scriptures in church life. Their proximity to New Testament origins did give a good grasp of the meaning and implications of the scriptures, and the quality of their work sprang from their attunement to the life and mission of the church. By focusing on the role of the New Testament in church ministries, we find ourselves consciously rejoining their various approaches.

What we have said concerning patristic interpretation in general also applies to the New Testament's interpretation of the Old. Its authors were not trying to understand Old Testament passages but their own life challenges. In doing so, they turned to the Old Testament for language and literary patterns. By the same token, they discovered the meaning of the Old Testament in the context of church life and ministry. Gospel writers like Matthew and Luke approached Mark, their literary source, in the same way. The interpretation of the Fathers was consequently in direct continuity with the New Testament's mode and nature of interpretation.

In its pastoral effort, as official documents attest, the church never lost sight of these approaches, and they continued to influence the church actively engaged in her mission. The scholarly efforts for understanding sprang from the scientific awareness and methods of modern times, and as such they represent a unique contribution of our era. However, as we consciously and explicitly focus on the New Testament in the church's ministries, we are also becoming aware of their limitations.

A good sense of history can help us to discern the issues, to situate ourselves with regard to the past, to discover the unique contribution of modern scholarship and to position our future efforts. For this, I would suggest a short, excellent book by Robert M. Grant, *A Short History of the Interpretation of the Bible* (New York: Macmillan paperbacks, revised edition, 1972). In this book, Grant provides a historical analysis of biblical interpretation and an insightful critique of many contemporary approaches. Beginning with Jesus' use of the Old Testament, he moves through the various historical periods all the way to modern Roman Catholic and Protestant interpretation.

For a more thorough historical look at modern times, there is also Stephen Neill's *The Interpretation of the New Testament 1861-1961* (London: Oxford University Press, 1966), a book born of a series of lectures (Firth Lectures) given at the University of Nottingham in November, 1962. The book focuses on the forms of New Testament criticism and presents these from the point of view of the various problems these mean to solve and the way scholars have perceived the task of interpretation.

In a series entitled *Guide to Biblical Scholarship* (Philadelphia), Fortress Press has published an excellent presentation of the various forms of contemporary New Testament criticism. Contributions to the series include Norman Perrin's *What Is Redaction Criticism?* (1969), Edgar V. McKnight's *What Is Form Criticism?* (1969), William A. Beardslee's *Literary Criticism of the New*

Testament (1970), and Edgar Kretz's *The Historical-Critical Method* (1975).

For a clear and simple exposition of the method of form criticism and its relationship to prior approaches, a long essay by Rudolf Bultmann, one of the creative minds who developed the method and applied it extensively, is extremely useful. It is entitled, "The Study of the Synoptic Gospels," and is found in a book entitled *Form Criticism, Two Essays on New Testament Research* (Willett: Clark and Company, 1934, and Harper Torchbooks, 1962).

An excellent and comprehensive treatment of the various methods of interpretation can be found in Daniel J. Harrington's *Interpreting the New Testament, a Practical Guide*, volume 1 of the 22-volume *New Testament Message*, a biblical-theological commentary published by Michael Glazier, Inc. (Wilmington, 1979). Harrington's purpose in this introductory volume is to provide beginners with an explanation of how the various methods used in the study of literature can be fruitfully employed in reading the New Testament. Each method is analyzed and its application to the New Testament scriptures explored.

Many have been writing on contemporary literary approaches to the New Testament. Among these, I would like to single out Amos N. Wilder's *Early Christian Rhetoric, the Language of the Gospel* (SCM Press Ltd., Harper and Row, 1964, and Cambridge, Massachusetts: Harvard University Press, 1971). From the same author, we have "The Symbolics of the New Testament," chapter IV of Part One in his *The New Voice, Religion, Literature, Hermeneutics* (New York: Herder and Herder, 1969), pp. 99-122. The author's sensitivity to literature, his own literary creativity, and his sense of the church as a factor in interpretation brings modern critical approaches to the very edge of active, communicative interpretation in the church.

An essay which might help those involved in ministry to see how the scholarly quest for understanding can contribute to interpretation in the communication process is my own "Literary Forms of the Bible," published in the study helps included in the *Good News Bible, the Bible in Today's English Version, Catholic Study Edition* (New York: Sadlier, 1979), pp. xlii-1.

A major source of our renewed sensitivity to the use of the New Testament in the life of the church comes from the Latin American theologians, men like Gustavo Gutierrez, Juan Luis Segundo, Leonardo Boff and Jon Sobrino. These authors, whose writings have been made available to the English-speaking world by Orbis Press (Maryknoll, New York), draw deeply from the New Testament to articulate and focus the church's mission to the Third World of Central and South America. Their work is being found universally relevant.

From the point of view of biblical scholarship, these authors have frequently been severely criticized, at times rightly, as they acknowledge, but most of the time inappropriately. Their task, and this is their unique contribution to contemporary theology, is to seek understanding not through mere reflection on our Christian heritage and the present-day life of the church but through the actual exercise of the church ministries as they are called forth by the social context. Their interpretation of the New Testament is thus ordained to communication and expression. Their emphasis is on praxis. If they are to be criticized, it is first and primarily on this ground and not on that of the various forms of biblical criticism.

Like the Fathers of the church, the "liberation theologians" as they are called turn to the scriptures to proclaim, articulate and express the life of the church. Their work is a challenge to us. This book takes up their challenge as it addresses the needs of the apostolic and pastoral life of the church. As in their case, it is limited by the scope of my experience as well as by any hesitations and fears of engaging fully in the church's mission. A quotation from Sobrino summarizes the challenge: "Following Jesus is the precondition for knowing Jesus" (*Christology at the Crossroads;* Maryknoll, New York: Orbis Press, 1978, p. xiii).

The New Testament in the Life of the Church

1
The New Testament in Evangelization

Evangelization is the most fundamental of all the ministries. Unless the Gospel has been proclaimed and unless it has been heard and accepted, every other ministry is futile. Without prior evangelization, catechesis falls on deaf ears, prophecy fails to rouse, the liturgy is Spiritless, homiletics finds no echo, spiritual direction has no anchor, the lamp of prayer is extinguished, and theology becomes a rational or historical exercise.

Such a fundamental ministry claims more than priority over the others. It permeates them as well. In a sense, every other ministry is an extension of evangelization into various aspects of Christian life and development. Born of the Gospel and enjoying its life, no ministry can afford to lose touch with its freshness and vitality.

Evangelization is thus a complex ministry, whose initial phase may be called primary evangelization, and whose later phases may be termed ongoing evangelization.

Evangelization is also the most simple of the ministries. Through it, a word of life is shared, people know that life is meaningful, that it is God's gift in Christ, and that it is a gift to be shared. Evangelization puts men and women in touch with their most profound human aspiration to live beyond every limitation of circumstance and history, and it places God's very own life

27

within their grasp. Evangelization unveils a promise and bestows the conviction that the promise is not empty. Shared in love, the promise is received in faith, and it is a gift of hope.

Fundamental and simple as evangelization is, no ministry is more demanding. Life is simple, faith direct, charity straightforward, and hope available to all. However, it takes the simplicity of a child to receive and share those Gospel values. It takes the maturity of an adult to achieve such simplicity. Only a true Christian can be an evangelist.

In modern times, the church has alerted all of us to the need for evangelization. Its appeal was born of awareness that the world is open to the Gospel and that it needs to hear it. It was born of another awareness as well, namely, that many of us take the Gospel for granted and, worse, that for many who claim the name Christian, its word has dissolved into a mere sound. Within our own church the Gospel must again be proclaimed, and the many who have barely heard it or accepted it with too many reservations must again hear it with all its life-giving and liberating power.

This call has been uttered in many ways. Its major statement, however, is the apostolic exhortation of Pope Paul VI, *Evangelii Nuntiandi*, "The Gospels Must Be Proclaimed," a message to the universal church which articulates the challenge of all Christians and the need of all human beings. The exhortation was issued from Vatican City on December 8, 1975. Its official English translation appeared in *The Pope Speaks* (1976) 21:4-51. Issued on the 10th anniversary of the close of Vatican II, as well as on the first anniversary of the general assembly of the synod of bishops which had been devoted to evangelization, the exhortation develops

28

many of the Council's concerns and reflects the mind of the synod. It also takes up the numerous statements of Paul VI himself on this subject and includes them in a comprehensive synthesis. Few would disagree that it constitutes one of the major contributions of Paul VI to the life of the church.

An important statement from the church in the United States is found in the National Catechetical Directory for Catholics of the United States. Entitled *Sharing the Light of Faith,* this directory was approved by the National Conference of Catholic Bishops at their general meeting of November 14-17, 1977, and approved by the Sacred Congregation for the Clergy, Second Office, on October 30, 1978. The relevant passage is in numbers 34 and 35, which present both pre-evangelization and evangelization as altogether indispensable for fruitful catechesis.

As in so many other areas, the impetus for Paul VI's call to evangelization sprang from Vatican Council II, which frequently turned to the question of evangelization. In *Lumen Gentium* (1964), the Dogmatic Constitution on the Church, but even more so in *Gaudium et spes* (1965), the Pastoral Constitution on the Church in the Modern World, the Council laid the groundwork for viewing the church as an agent of evangelization. The strongest, most highly developed statement on the subject, however, is the decree *Ad gentes divinitus* (1965), which bears on the church's missionary activity.

One of the very significant points emphasized in these documents is that evangelization is a task of all the members of the church and not only of those in sacred orders. Accordingly, another key conciliar document on evangelization is the decree *Apostolicam actuositatem* (1965), which treats of the apostolate of lay people.

Since evangelization is the mission of all in the church, it must be approached as an apostolic ministry in itself and as a function of the church as such, not as the special vocation of those who have fully devoted themselves to its task. With this perspective, all who take up the church's mission of evangelization in the New Testament are seen as models for us all and not as men and women set apart from the rest of us.

The Witness of the New Testament

To say New Testament is to say Gospel, and to say Gospel is to say evangelization. While the New Testament works were not written as texts for evangelization, they presuppose it throughout and frequently refer to the origins of Christianity in the Gospel mission of Jesus and the early church. This is true, of course, of the four narratives which we now call Gospels and of the Acts of the Apostles, which is Luke's second volume. It is also true of other works and preeminently of Paul's letters to churches and individuals. For the witness of the New Testament, we consequently turn to evangelization in the story of Jesus, in that of the church and in the letters of Paul.

Jesus   In Luke 4:18-19, Jesus' entire life is presented as a mission of evangelization. That is why he has been anointed and why consequently he is the Christ. That is also why the Spirit of the Lord is upon him. Proclaimed to a human race which is in fact poor in relation to God's imperishable wealth, and whose genuinely and socially poor are living sacraments or symbols of this

30

common poverty, the Gospel word can be spelled out as release for captives, recovery of sight for the blind and liberty for the oppressed.

In the Lukan text, Jesus himself presents this message and applies it to his person and mission in the Nazareth synagogue (4:21) and in the greater Gentile world (4:23-27). His language, however, is drawn from the book of Isaiah, and especially from 61:1-2, 58:6 and 42:7. In keeping with the general tenor of Isaiah, these texts emphasize the universality of Israel's Gospel mission. Jesus thus fulfills the vocation of Israel to bring the Gospel to all, and the evangelization mission is deeply rooted in Old Testament tradition and literature.

When Luke wrote, Mark had already summarized Jesus' mission as preaching the Gospel of God and he had outlined the content of his preaching as the fulfillment of times with the approach of the kingdom of God. Jesus' hearers were thus to repent and believe in the Gospel (1:14-15).

Like Luke 4:18-19, Mark's summary statement and the Gospel synthesis which he credits to Jesus are also drawn from Isaiah. The principal passage is 40:9-10, in which Zion or Jerusalem is a herald or proclaimer of the Good News that the Lord God comes to rule with might. Jesus thus fulfills the promise of the scriptures, and his evangelizing mission echoes the depths of a tradition from which it derives strength even in its newness and in his unique realization of the prophetic promise.

The Church   The summaries of Luke and Mark, as well as many others, are significant as expressions of Jesus' mission, which the Gospels present as a model statement of the church's own task in the world. The texts cited concerning Jesus, important as they are, indicate only part of the Gospel. In the works of Mark, Luke and others, they are supplemented by many episodes which draw out their implications. Some of these, namely the passion and resurrection narratives, were not part of Jesus' message but its ultimate implications. For the church, the radical and unflinching quality of Jesus' commitment to evangelization becomes absolutely plain in the passion event, an event which God crowned with resurrection. In the resurrection, God gave life to one who gave it and through him to all who are willing to join him in offering their lives that captives might be released, the blind might see and the oppressed be set free. In Christ, the risen Lord, the church extends the mission of the historical Jesus beyond his death into its own history.

The early New Testament church thus set Jesus' passion-resurrection at the core of the Good News. In this, it did not neglect the message of Jesus but proclaimed it in light of its most profound significance. The Good News concerning Jesus thus provided the context for every other expression of the Good News of God which Jesus had proclaimed.

In the New Testament, the book of Acts provides our clearest and most direct witness to the church's mission of evangelization. We find it primarily in the speeches of Peter and in the speeches and work of Paul, which are grounded in those of Peter, Jesus' first disciple (Lk 5:1-11) and the first to see the risen Lord (Lk 24:34). In these speeches, what Jesus said and did is either briefly indicated or merely evoked by a reference to Jesus of Nazareth. The apostolic focus is rather on the passion-resurrection and how these called all to repentance and faith.

Paul The early Church was blessed with many outstanding evangelists. None of these, however, has left us a written witness to his work which is comparable to Paul's. Paul's letters presuppose that those he is addressing have been evangelized. Of their nature, they are thus examples of the catechetical or teaching and prophetic functions of the church. They can also be viewed, at least in many instances, as examples of ongoing evangelization.

Although Paul's letters cannot be classed as texts intended for primary evangelization, they do frequently refer to the moments when he first approached the community with the Good News, to the content of his message and to the Christian response to it. They can thus be viewed as texts about primary evangelization. It is from this point of view that we approach them as we focus on Paul's witness to the mission of evangelization.

Paul viewed himself primarily as an apostle of Christ Jesus who was set apart to proclaim the Gospel of God. This awareness is inscribed, with varying degrees of explicitness, in the introductory address of his letters. Accordingly, whatever might be his special purpose in writing, his message is always linked to the community's origins in the Gospel's proclamation. Consequently, the communities are never allowed to lose sight of the basic values which give meaning to any other consideration of life, faith and mission.

This relationship between later concerns and initial evangelization is especially evident in those letters where the foundation Gospel message and its intended results appeared threatened.

In 1 and 2 Thessalonians, the earliest of Paul's letters (circa 51-52 A.D.), the threat had come from persecutions, and Paul writes to express his thanksgiving that in spite of these the Christians of the Macedonian capital were steadfast and flourishing. He thus reviews the history of the community's evangelizing and deals with any problems which have surfaced from this point of view.

In Galatians (circa 54 A.D.), he argues against deviations from the Gospel's purity. Some were retreating to pre-Christian norms of life and requiring that all, whether Jew or Gentile, be subjected to the Law. Paul recalls the freedom which the Galatian Christians had first acquired from the Gospel's proclamation and asks that they be faithful to the Gospel's abrogation of all legal prescriptions. In Christ, the distinction between Jew and Gentile no longer obtained.

In 1 and 2 Corinthians (circa 56-57 A.D.), Paul reaffirms the absolute value of the initial Gospel proclamation and attacks any efforts to set it aside in favor of further teaching given by visiting Christians or sprung from the community's own reflection on basic issues. In the social context, his response to the situation frequently takes the form of an apologetic for his apostolic mission in Corinth. Since the Corinthian correspondence deals so extensively with problems arising from the relationship between evangelization and catechesis, the subject of my second chapter, these reflections on the Pauline witness will focus on these letters and more particularly on 1 Corinthians 1:10-4:21.

In the first part of 1 Corinthians, 1:10-6:20, Paul deals with a report brought to him by members of Chloe's household (1:10-4:21) and other matters which have reached him by word of mouth (5:1-13; 6:1-20). In the first section the problem lies in the community's

34

reaction to a well-educated and dedicated Christian who had followed Paul's long stay at Corinth and had propounded the Christian message in language and concepts which were far more sophisticated than Paul's and more palatable than his simple Gospel message. Many had rallied around this man's name, Apollos, and had disassociated themselves from Paul and his proclamation of the Gospel. Others remained faithful to Paul and rallied around his name. In the confusion and divisions, other names, such as Cephas and Christ, also had been reduced to mere slogans, verbal banners and rallying cries for a seriously divided and factious community (1:10-12; 3:3-4).

Addressing this situation, Paul sets aside all secondary considerations and strikes at the heart of the matter. Paul had preached the basic Gospel message with simplicity and power. That message bore on the cross of Christ (1:13-17; 2:1-5), a cross mirrored in the weakness and lowly origins of the Corinthians (1:26-31) as well as in Paul's own weakness, fear and trembling (2:1-3). Paul's preaching was thus the paradox of the cross in which human weakness and folly are divine power and wisdom (1:18-25).

In metaphorical language, Paul states that his evangelization of Corinth had laid the foundations and planted the seed. Apollos, a servant with a different but complementary mission, had watered the seed and started to build on the Pauline foundation (3:5-9). Unless this relationship was recognized and unless those who built erected the building on the original foundation, namely the cross of Christ, all building was in vain (3:10-15).

The Gospel of the cross is a radical message, which

overturns so-called human values, institutions and structures and transforms them into the kingdom of God. It works for a divine order in which humanity realizes its true self by acknowledging its nothingness before God.

At Thessalonica and Galatia, the Gospel of God in Christ our Lord struck at the divisions between Jews and Gentiles and affirmed the Gospel's leveling and uniting demands. For the Thessalonians this had led to resistance and attacks from the synagogue and its leaders as well as from the Gentiles and the political rulers (see Acts 17:1-9). Paul's Jewish accusers were right in their claim that Paul and Silas were turning the world upside down (Acts 17:6). For the Galatians, it had eventually led to resistance in the community itself, whose members had to discover a new personal identity in which being Jew or Gentile, slave or free, male or female was of no import (Gal 3:28). Relationships in a community where all are one in Christ Jesus could not be based on these historical, social and biological distinctions. If so, however, would not the very distinctions actually disappear, at least in the manner of relating and in their incorporation in social structures and church life?

At Corinth, the Gospel struck at the order of human wisdom and all false values which flowed from it. The only wisdom which ultimately fulfilled those who pursued it was that which assumed the cross to the point of being willing to die for the sake of others. A world which would be so imbued with selflessness and commitment to others is vastly different from a selfish world of pretense, search for security, personal accumulation and divisiveness.

36

Proclaiming the New Testament's Gospel

In terms of the New Testament and its use, evangelization can be divided into four stages, primary evangelization and three stages of ongoing evangelization. These last three stages I refer to as the quest for consistency, the search for a synthesis and the integration of ambiguity.

First, there is primary or initial evangelization. In the beginnings of Gospel proclamation and sharing, we present the simple core of the message and tell its stories in such a way that our hope and our stories become those of others.

Like life itself, the Gospel is first communicated through a human encounter and not through a literary work or a letter which articulates it or develops its ramifications. As in the case of Jesus and the earliest church, the Gospel we proclaim is fundamentally our own life, the life of God in us or our life in Christ. For this we need language, of course, language which has been inspired by the New Testament but which has become our own word. The word of primary evangelization springs from a human experience penetrated by the Spirit of God and Christ. At this first stage of evangelization, it is consequently not appropriate to use the literary text of the New Testament. Like Paul, our Gospel proclamation must be that of personal presence and the living word.

In the second stage of evangelization, we join the initially evangelized in a Christian quest for consistency in faith and practice. At this stage, we proceed to draw out the implications of the Gospel which our listeners have simply but profoundly internalized. We now begin to use the New Testament texts. In doing so, however, we are careful to select texts which correspond to the level of development which the initially evangelized have attained. Among these, the Pauline texts which reiterate the simple Gospel message and spell out its requirements seem most appropriate.

In the third stage, we come to grips with the maturing Christian's need for a Christian life synthesis. It does not suffice to be consistent in several major areas of concern. The many aspects of life must be seen as an integrated whole in which values are hierarchically interrelated. For this we take up one or another of the Gospel syntheses such as we have in the Gospel narratives and in some of the major New Testament letters. As in the previous stage, it matters that we select a synthesis which corresponds to the personal and social situation of those being evangelized.

In the fourth stage, we address the mature Christian's need to recognize and accept the various polarities and tensions which characterize adult faith and Christian life in the church community. All do not share the same fundamental Gospel synthesis, and indeed no synthesis is fully adequate for the individual Christian's own personal life. At this stage we consequently examine the entire New Testament with its multiplicity of syntheses and its numerous statements on special questions affecting Christian life.

In the following pages, I shall examine how the New Testament can appropriately be used in proclaiming the Gospel at each of the stages I have outlined.

Stage 1: Primary Evangelization   For those involved in evangelization, and we all must be, the most fundamental interpretation of the New Testament cannot be in words at all, however holy or divine, but in life. The quality of the proclaimer's life is the primary interpretation of the Gospel. In contemporary language, we would say that the ultimate hermeneutic is the Christian person. At this level, we can also say that the object of evangelization is to call forth human beings to Christ's life so that they too become living interpretations of the New Testament. This process, which Paul alluded to in terms of imitation, is the basic substructure of tradition, through which the Gospel is borne through the course of history and into every social context.

Jesus himself was such an interpreter of the Gospel. As he presented himself, people were aware that they encountered more than a Jew from Nazareth. His impact raised the question of his identity: "Is not this Joseph's son?" (Lk 4:22). His word was different and spoken with the authority of the Gospel which penetrated his entire person (Lk 4:36). So must it be with the Christian evangelist.

John described Jesus as the Word, that is the Word of God become flesh (1:14). The goal of the Christian evangelist is to approximate Jesus' fleshing out of God's Gospel word. To become so we must assume his commitment to the life of our fellow human beings even to the point of death. To the extent that we do so our personal hermeneutic of the Gospel will share the authority of Jesus himself.

As living Gospel interpretations, we can then speak the Gospel. To do so effectively, however, our initial proclamation must remain close to early Christian practice. The apostolic church and the second generation of evangelists, which was composed of men and women the likes of Paul, did not have extensive Gospel narratives to share. They spoke simply and directly of the most essential realities, and they addressed these to the needs and unfulfilled hopes of those who crossed their path or to whom they went. Their message spoke of life where everything shouted death, and for this they turned to the ultimate implications of Jesus' mission, that is, to his death and resurrection.

This is a difficult and uncompromising approach. To be credible the early evangelists had to bear the stamp of Jesus' death and resurrection. Their very lives proclaimed the death and resurrection of Jesus, and when their hearers heard them speak of these, they believed because the message was alive first of all in them and only secondarily in the verbal medium through which they communicated it.

Taking this approach, we proclaim the Gospel of the cross and resurrection first without the elaboration of its implications for various life situations and without spelling out all of its doctrinal and ethical demands for faith and life. Were we to do otherwise, those to whom we are sent would be overwhelmed. Without the initial faith commitment to love and hope, they would have no basis on which to see the more extensive teaching as the logical consequence of the Gospel. The initial interiorization of the Gospel is essential for all genuine development, whose norm must be a word inscribed in the heart. Otherwise, verbal assent might be given, but without the conviction which transforms the believer into one who proclaims the Gospel with authority. For such a one, the word would be extrinsic, the eye would not be opened in faith, and knowledge would not spring from the committed Christian self but from a word inscribed on tablets of stone or in a book.

Sensitive to the life context of those who first heard the Gospel, the evangelist then proceeds to flesh out the

Gospel concretely with stories told by Jesus or told about him. These stories assure the Gospel's relevance to the concrete situations in which the Gospel is heard. As in Jesus' life, those who hear the Gospel are poor and rich people, tax collectors and prostitutes, centurions and soldiers, Pharisees and priests, young and old. Finding themselves in the audiences Jesus addressed, people can thus hear the core of the Gospel message as spoken to them and not to privileged but merely imagined audiences.

A Gospel story is effective in evangelization when it is told as a story thoroughly assimilated by the evangelist. A story which is merely read and which remains someone else's story is not effective. The evangelist must possess the story, like we possess so many other stories, must want to tell it because it burns within him or her and wants to be told, and must tell it to the particular people being addressed. For this to be possible, the story must be so much a part of the evangelist that attention focuses altogether on the one or the many to whom it is told. As in all storytelling, the changing response of the hearers determines what should be emphasized, further developed or explained.

This approach to telling the story has obvious dangers. The storyteller might have a poor grasp of the story as it is found in the New Testament. He or she can also get carried away by personal fancy. Evangelization might then have a high degree of personal authenticity from the point of view of the evangelist, but it would not present the Gospel of the church as a whole. To counter such difficulties, extensive catechesis is needed, and such is the purpose of the many programs directed to adult evangelists in the church. Conducted in group or ecclesial settings, these programs help the Christian to grow as a member of the universal church. Only in this way can we guarantee that the faith of the Christian evangelist is the faith of the church.

The first stage of evangelization clearly applies to those who have not yet heard the Gospel, but it also applies to those who already are members of the church, who may have been baptized as infants, but in whom the Gospel word is taken for granted, remains mute and has never been consciously appropriated. With such as these, however, the task is even more difficult, since they learned to accept Christian realities as facts of life. The church provides part of the personal supports and the points of reference so necessary for fashioning their human identity and for maintaining feelings of inner security in a complex and changing world.

In these circumstances, the evangelist must be able to penetrate the barriers of familiarity to awaken the spark of Gospel excitement and creativity. The direct communication of the simple Gospel message and a personally involved storyteller goes a long way toward overcoming the acquired sense of blandness, however long established.

To this point I have emphasized how the person of the evangelist and the Gospel's simple interiorized message are fundamental for interpretation in the evangelization process. Those with whom the Gospel is shared also contribute to its interpretation. The Christian commitment and the cross find their meaning in Jesus and his followers, the evangelists of every age. Suffering and the human condition which these address, however, are also the lot of those to whom we are sent. Evangelists must be open to being evangelized by those with whom they try to share the Gospel. No one is ever

42

really an evangelist unless he or she is also the evangelized.

Accordingly, the evangelists come to understand the Gospel's message concerning suffering, death and new life through the life-realities of their hearers. As the evangelized accept the Gospel, they become living interpretations of the Gospel and an experiential point of reference for understanding the Gospel of Christ. The Gospel is thus grasped not as a set of concepts and notions but in its articulation of a human life which is open to the way of Christ. The blind, the lame, the oppressed, the enslaved and the poor are all around us. The meaning of these terms is drawn not only from their ancient historical and philological contests but from their living exemplars which we encounter daily.

Stage 2: The Quest for Consistency   Once the Gospel has been planted, the plant needs to be watered (see 1 Cor 3:5-9). Life is developmental and complex in its relationships. Unless the Gospel reaches into all of its phases and spheres, evangelization will remain ineffectual. It will be like the seed which sprang up in shallow soil or which grew among thorns. Scorched by the sun of life's challenges, it fast withers. Choked by the thorns, it clings to life but yields nothing (Mk 4:5-7).

Evangelization must consequently pursue the implications of the Gospel for every area of life. In this it appeals to the basic grasp of the death and resurrection of Jesus, takes up the various spheres of commitment and belief and calls people to a faith expression and a mode of life which are consistent with their new or renewed Christian self.

Beginning with this stage, evangelization overlaps

materially with catechesis or teaching. In the New Testament, the respective terms for these are *kerygma* and *didache*. From the point of view of content, these may be the same. However, to preach or share the Gospel is not the same as to teach or facilitate understanding. It is true, of course, that evangelization includes a measure of catechesis and vice versa. Concretely, the difference lies in one's emphasis and purpose.

At this second stage, the evangelist can turn to various passages in Paul's letters and especially to units which begin by reaffirming the basic Gospel statement and commitment and which draw out its implications. Two kinds of passages are particularly useful, those which bear on attitudes and behavior and those which address matters of belief. The two, of course, are intimately related. Belief has consequences for living; ethical practice, both personal and social, has consequences for belief. Faith is part of life, and the quality of Christian life is an expression of faith. The two are nevertheless distinguishable for purposes of evangelization.

As in primary evangelization, this second stage focuses on the people we mean to evangelize. Now, however, these people are Christians, men and women who have faced life's creaturely limitations and mortality and who have embraced new divine life as they look to its fullness in God. Christ's death and resurrection provide the pattern for their existence, and they have accepted that their lives be the human sacrament of his death and resurrection. With Mary, they have responded to God's call with a personal "Let it be done to me according to your word" (Lk 1:38).

Ongoing evangelization first addresses the Christians in their need to live as Christians. For this purpose,

44

passages like 1 Corinthians 10:1-3 and 1 Corinthians 11:17-34 prove extremely useful.

The baptism and the spiritual food and drink of which Paul speaks in 1 Corinthians 10:2-4 are interpreted through their own baptismal and eucharistic experience. These sacraments represent the needed point of reference for bringing Paul's exodus references to meaningful expression, and the Old Testament events become symbolic statements which evoke Christian baptism and Eucharist not only in themselves but more concretely as these have been known and lived by Paul's listeners and ours.

This relationship between Paul's New Testament naming of Old Testament events and the lived experience of the evangelized is a critical element in using the text for evangelization purposes. As the evangelists proceed, the meaning of the text unfolds gradually through its resonance in the Christians and in the quality of their appreciation of their own baptism and Eucharist. To the extent that their baptism and Eucharist were deeply and authentically Christian, the contribution of these to the interpretation of the text will be meaningful and valid. To the extent that they held little or no meaning for them or distorted meaning, the text will not be appropriately interpreted and its use ineffectual.

Once the Old Testament events have truly become the images of Christian baptism and Eucharist, we can appreciate what Paul wishes to say concerning them. Baptism and Eucharist mediate the Lord's life and presence to Christians and are salvific. However, Christians cannot rest secure in that salvific presence as though sin were no longer a possibility for them and the fullness of life were already acquired. Baptism and

Eucharist are also human responses to life's challenges as disclosed by God in primary evangelization and its sacramental consummation. Commitment to values and attitudes and to living and dying that others might live is an essential component of baptism and Eucharist. If these sacramental events are to persist as experiences of salvation, they must also be commitments to the church's saving mission.

What the commitment requires will be spelled out by the concrete personal and social contexts of those being evangelized, and these become part of the interpretation of what it means to avoid idolatry (10:7), lewd indulgence (10:8) and grumbling (10:10). In evangelization, the text's meaning is thus drawn largely from the communication context and not exclusively from an exegetical analysis of its meaning for Paul and those he addresses or even from a hermeneutical analysis of its meaning for another situation. Experience, and not the text, is the point of departure. In this approach, the text becomes the vehicle for articulating our contemporary challenges, and these challenges are situated in their Gospel context and struck through with the power of God's word. In the process, our experience is measured by the New Testament. The text is thus an objective norm, even as it is illumined by our experience.

In 1 Corinthians 11:17-34, we have an example similar to that of 1 Corinthians 10. The ancient liturgical text for the Lord's Supper (11:23-25), a text which evokes the acceptance of primary evangelization, which highlights the betrayal which accompanied Jesus' Last Supper and which interprets his death as accepted for the salvation of all, raises the question of ongoing betrayals in the Christian community. These betrayals

46

are especially evident in the community's assembly for the Lord's Supper.

Paul shows how such betrayals, which loom large in the participants' social and economic inequities and unwillingness to share (11:17-22), are inconsistent with lives which should reflect the attitudes of Jesus and are meant to proclaim the death of the Lord in history until he comes (11:26). In evangelization, the meaning of the text arises from the existing betrayals of the community, betrayals which may be only analogous to those of Corinth, but which are just as inconsistent with the Lord's Supper. Unless such betrayals are eliminated, the evangelized cannot be genuine evangelists (11:26-34).

Ongoing evangelization also addresses the Christians in their need to believe as Christians. The ancient creed (1 Corinthians 15:3b-5), for example, has implications for belief in other but related matters. Failure to be consistent can nullify the simple creed's primary affirmation of faith. Such is Paul's argument in 1 Corinthians 15.

As in 1 Corinthians 10:1-13 and 11:17-34, the meaning of the creed itself depends on the life of those who profess it and not only on the conclusions of exegesis and hermeneutics. The pronoun "our" and the word "sins" which it modifies in 15:3b make this absolutely clear. What is important is not so much what Paul meant by sins or what the term as term means in our own time, but our very own sins, whatever they may be, and the way they qualify and limit our lives in specific social contexts with whatever personal and communal responsibilities are ours.

In 1 Corinthians 15:1-58, Paul insists that belief in Christ's resurrection requires belief in our own. To deny our own is to deny the very purpose of Christ's. To this end, he argues against every effort to deny the resurrection of Christians and tries to correct any presuppositions which stand in the way of belief and hope. The questions raised by the Corinthians are our own, but as invested with the peculiar sophistication and attitudes of our time.

Stage 3: The Search for a Synthesis   Although the process of adult human development is complex, it does include a number of recognizable stages which are universally meaningful. Each of these stages is initiated and permeated by a set of challenges which must be met for further development.

At some given moment, a young person, for example, awakens to personal life, consciously assumes it and makes a commitment to it. In the ensuing months or even years, it becomes necessary for the youth to explore the particular implications of this experience and commitment. This exploration is pursued as he or she is thrust out of the family community of birth and early development into expanded relationships, concerns and responsibilities. Eventually, however, there comes a moment when a distinct need is felt to bring all these elements together and to place the various aspects and responsibilities in perspective. This is the challenge and the moment of synthesis. Secondary facets are subordinated to the primary, a conscious hierarchy of values is established, and life acquires both focus and direction.

Adult Christian development follows a like course, and so must the process of evangelization. In primary evangelization, a Christian awakens to Gospel values and commitment. There follows a period of exploration and application as one moves with the Gospel into the various spheres of adult life and responsibility. I have referred to this period as the quest for consistency. Sooner or later, however, this quest becomes transformed into a search for a Christian life synthesis. Without such a synthesis, Christian life would appear disorganized, and the mission which it entails would remain sporadic and without the power to follow through which characterized the life of Jesus.

We have already explored how the New Testament influences the first stage and can be appropriately applied and interpreted in the second stage of evangelization. In the third stage, we move beyond the Gospel's simple expression and its first implications for life and faith, and we turn to the great Gospel syntheses of Mark, Matthew, Luke and John.

In the evangelization process, we should not attempt to interiorize these syntheses until the need for a personal synthesis has emerged out of the prior stages and is clearly felt. Without such a need, the Gospel narratives might prove interesting, but they would fall on deaf ears, they would not serve the mission of evangelization, and their own purpose would be frustrated.

Each of the Gospels represents a distinct synthesis of Christian life arising from a particular set of circumstances, a concrete stance of the church in relation to these circumstances at a given period in its own development, and a major Christian figure's response to the Gospel mission in his time. These syntheses can help maturing Christians to formulate and judge their own emerging synthesis of Christian life.

While the Gospels are far from identical syntheses, they do have a number of elements in common which are relevant to New Testament interpretation in the evangelization process. Among these, the most significant may be their focus on vision and mission, the distinction between these and their relationship.

Each of the Gospel narratives of Jesus' life and mission includes a major statement of vision from which all else springs. These coincide with Jesus' baptism (Mk 1:9-11; Mt 3:13-17), are associated with it (Lk 3:21-22) or supplant it (John 1:31-34). At the core of these vision statements, the authors present the ultimate meaning of Jesus' life and mission, and the latter is shown to spring from the creative Spirit of God.

With these brief narratives, the authors alert us to the danger of losing our way in a forest of issues and concerns and of losing sight of our initial proclamation or acceptance of the Gospel. Therein lies our vision. As in Jesus' case, it is the energizing source and the dynamism which bind every aspect of life into a vital synthesis. Without it, we become mere church functionaries, busy perhaps, but without Spirit.

The same Gospel narratives show how Jesus' vision was channeled into a mission. Unless the vision had found expression in a concrete mission which responded to the needs of men and women in his time, it would have become ultimately meaningless and vain and a source of enormous frustration. In our own times, we have all met Christians with vision but no mission. They are exciting people, full of energy, potential and grand projects. Unfortunately, however, these never seem to flow into responsibilities and a vocational commitment such as the social apostolate. Taken by a vision, as indeed they should be, they are unable to accept their own limited possibilities for contributing to its realization. The visionary flame either dies or becomes a consuming and self-destructive fire.

Each of the Gospels also includes a vision in which Jesus' followers are challenged by the power of the Gospel and sent on a mission. These are found in the accounts of visits to Jesus' tomb and the appearances of the risen Lord, all of which apply the vision and mission of Jesus to those of Christians in light of the passion and resurrection event.

In the case of both Jesus and the Christians, the vision which calls for heroic commitment can be expressed in terms of the kingdom of God. The mission is the particular task to preach, teach, heal, reconcile and baptize in view of the vision's fulfillment.

As we take up the Gospel syntheses in evangelization, we do well to consider how vision and mission have been integrated in them. To interpret them, we must ask how those being evangelized have experienced the vision and how their mission is gradually being clarified. With this point of departure, all further use of the Gospels will prove exciting and pertinent.

As was indicated, the Gospels hold many elements in common. However, each is also a unique synthesis. The second task is consequently to select a Gospel which is appropriate for the life synthesis of a particular set of hearers. While each could serve this purpose, not all are equally appropriate.

Mark's Gospel (circa 70 A.D.) addressed communities of Christians who were threatened by the disintegration of the world as they had known it. Thrust into an inhospitable political environment, whose military might had destroyed Jerusalem and the Judean cradle of its origins, the Markan community found little hope in the future and felt its mission energy drained. Many members looked to an apocalyptic resolution of the present age and a divine intervention which would install the kingdom in an endless and trouble-free future. Mark responded by emphasizing the radical commitment of the cross and calling the community to the Spirit which had first led it to proclaim the Gospel.

In situations where political and economic oppression is crippling and nearly overwhelming and in which the tendency to apocalyptic escapism is on the rise, Mark's Gospel seems to provide the most useful synthesis. His unflinching call to take up the cross and follow Jesus (8:34-38), his presentation of baptism and Eucharist as a commitment to Jesus' own bath of pain and to the cup of suffering which he would drink (10:35-45), and his proclamation of life in the midst of all the signs of death (16:1-8) can help struggling Christians to work for a divine kingdom which reduces earthly kingdoms to nothing.

Matthew's Gospel (circa 85 A.D.) addressed Jewish Christians who had recently been denied their ongoing relationship to the synagogue. From a Jewish point of view, they could no longer consider themselves as good and faithful Jews while maintaining their allegiance to Christ. This had disrupted families, placed all the members before a clear decision and turned the community outward into the Gentile environment. The community thus groped for a new point of reference to formulate its identity. Many tended to turn inwardly on themselves as they looked yearningly to the Judaism they loved, which flowed in their veins and which had enriched them with so many traditions which they had found liberating. Matthew responded by showing how Christianity constituted a new Israel with a mission to all the nations, a community in which Christians had to place love for Christ above every other love.

In situations where enormous changes have radically altered the stance of a cohesive church *vis-a-vis* the greater social and religious environment, Matthew's Gospel seems most appropriate for formulating a Gospel synthesis. His sense of community identity and the need for fidelity calls the evangelized to maintain clear distinctions between what is and what is not authentically Christian and to reach out to the world from a position of inner strength.

Luke's Gospel (circa 85 A.D.) addressed Gentile Christians whose communities were beset by persecutions from the outside and a host of problems from within. The internal problems were particularly evident in the community assemblies, in the sharing of goods with the needy and in the exercise of leadership. How did this situation come about? It hardly seemed possible that this was the promise which Jesus had held out to them. Many questioned whether the Gentile communities might not have moved so far away from their Jewish point of departure that they no longer represented authentic Christianity. Luke responded by writing a pastoral theology of early Christian history in which he traced the lines of continuity between Jesus, the risen Lord, the apostolic community and the Gentile mission. His basic principle for historical analysis and interpretation was that of promise and fulfillment.

In situations where the church stands in need of major renewal, where it finds itself challenged by new social developments and an expanding mission, and where many find it difficult to let go of past structures, Luke's two volumes, Luke-Acts, seem most appropriate for formulating a personal synthesis. His sense of continuity in the midst of change releases the energies of the evangelized for the Christian mission. Their own renewal keeps pace with their outreach to the world.

John's Gospel (circa 90 A.D.) addressed Christians whose view of Jesus was gradually emptying the Son of God of all humanity. Their understanding of who Jesus was was clearly related to their own self-understanding. The tendency was to approach Christianity in purely spiritual terms and to relegate all earthly things to the realm of darkness, a realm at war with the light of Christ. They were thus straying from the basic sacramental understanding of creation and salvation history whereby earthly life and realities were symbols capable of communicating the divine. John responded by roundly affirming that the Word of God was made flesh and by spelling out the consequences of this for the major areas of Christian living.

In situations where Christian life has lost touch with earthly concerns, where religion has become a purely spiritual relationship with the Lord, and where Christians do little to bring the Word of God into the fleshly realities of the world through which they make their way to salvation, John's Gospel appears most appropriate. His sense of the goodness of created things and humanity allows us to view ourselves, our neighbor and the world about us as symbols or sacraments through which God reveals himself and extends salvation.

Stage 4: The Integration of Ambiguity   Each of the Gospels is suited for evangelization at the point where Christians feel the need for coordinating life's many facets and formulating a synthesis. This synthesis, however, is not the ultimate stage in adult maturation. At a further stage, one must deal effectively with diversity in the church as well as with the polarities, tensions and resultant ambiguities in one's own life. The fourth stage of evangelization addresses these social and personal tensions and deals with the integration of ambiguity. At this stage the evangelist utilizes the entire New Testament.

Social diversity in the church is evident from the fact that not all have the same needs or face the same challenges and responsibilities. For some, Mark may have provided the needed synthesis; for others, Matthew, Luke or John, or even some other work which we did not consider. Were we to approach the New Testament purely from the point of view of its individual works, how would we help a Markan Christian, for example, to understand and accept a Johannine Christian? Would we not be encouraging at least a measure of sectarian divisiveness? In a universal church, can we afford to think in terms of Markan, Matthean, Lukan and Johannine Christians?

Experience also shows that each of us is a very complex person and hence a very complex Christian. Can any one Gospel synthesis be fully adequate to our reality? Once we have formulated our Christian existence in terms of Mark, for example, do we not find ourselves drawn to other Gospels or letters which reveal and formulate our Christian selves differently? It is possible, of course, to deny such polarities and tensions within ourselves, to become rigid and to refuse to cope with the ambiguity of Christian life. Such an attitude is usually translated into the rejection of those who are different from ourselves. More fundamentally, however, it rejects the challenge of personal development. The consequences are enormous. Arrested in development, the Christian loses his or her sense of Gospel freedom, the vision fades, and any role of leadership in the community becomes a struggle or even impossible.

The New Testament is more than a collection of disparate literary works from which one picks according to personal or immediate social need. The church accepts it as a whole which is capable of responding to the complex and diverse needs of both persons and communities. It is from this point of view that we now examine how it can be appropriately used at the fourth stage of evangelization.

The best point of departure at this fourth stage of evangelization is the personal Gospel synthesis of the persons addressed. In this way, one who has achieved an integrated life vision and mission according to St. Mark, for example, is able to approach other Gospel syntheses from a position of strength. The integration of ambiguity is thus achieved from a clearly defined but open-ended point of reference.

The alternative is to risk disorientation and general confusion. Without a personalized Gospel criterion, it becomes extremely difficult to launch into the unknown and to appreciate how the different Gospels are complementary and not incompatible syntheses of Christian life.

With one's Gospel synthesis as a point of departure, one can then take up another Gospel synthesis and see how it expressed the same vision and mission for a new time or a new Christian situation *vis-a-vis* the world. If Mark was actually the Gospel which provided our first synthesis, either of the other two synoptic Gospels provides a smooth second step. Matthew or Luke should be studied and presented as an interpretation of Mark for a new context. This interpretation involved extensive rewriting and a considerable expansion of the short Markan text through the assimilation of other traditions preserved in the life of the communities. In each case, the result was a new Gospel synthesis to be approached in its own right.

In studying the later synoptics, it is wise to pay special attention to the infancy and appearance narratives, both of which are unique to these Gospels. It is here that their greatest differences from Mark are most carefully spelled out. As the Christian recognizes that Mark's resurrection account—which mentions only the women's visit to the tomb (16:1-8)—presupposed a resurrection experience or appearance, it becomes clear that the appearance narratives at the end of Matthew and Luke articulate aspects of our Gospel synthesis which had remained implicit. The same is true of the infancy narratives, which present the entire Gospel in miniature and indicate the deeper implications of what it meant to be Jesus. In so doing, they show how Christology is related to biblical tradition, to the course of Jesus' mission and to what God brought about for the human race through his death and resurrection.

Special attention should also be paid to the sayings and discourses of Jesus. Mark had included some of these, but they play a relatively modest role in his Gospel. In the Gospels of Matthew and Luke, their place is greatly expanded. Through them, we can see the richness of the events in Jesus' life and the implications which they had for a variety of contexts. Mark, on the other hand, had shown but a few of those implications. By using the traditions of Jesus' teaching and preaching rather than their own reflections, Matthew and Luke endowed their Gospel syntheses with the authority of Jesus' teaching. They showed us how to plunge deeper into tradition when we are required to respond to new and unforeseen circumstances.

After broadening our base from Mark to one of the later synoptic Gospels, we might then focus our attention on the two later synoptics themselves. Since Matthew and Luke were contemporaries (circa 85 A.D.), a comparison of the way in which the history of their communities and differing social contexts called for distinct approaches to the rewriting and development of the Markan Gospel will prove very enlightening. The Gospel of Matthew was written for a community of Jewish origin which had recently been thrust out of Judaism and which was newly challenged by the Gentile world. It could not be written like the Gospel of Luke, which was addressed mainly to Gentiles coping with the many difficulties of adjustment to a political and economic world which continually challenged the Gospel's values. For Luke's readers, Judaism was not an object of recent or daily confrontation but an important element in the story of their origins.

After studying the synoptics, we can expand our horizon to include John's Gospel. Its concern with Jesus' origins in the eternal word of God and with his life and teaching as an incarnate expression of that word, is not unlike Luke's interest in the history of the word which came to John the Baptist, which was spoken by Jesus and which must spread to the ends of the earth through the life of the Christian community. Luke, however, approached the word in historical and prophetic terms. John was more profoundly influenced by Israel's tradition of wisdom. He thus helps us to relate the Christian story to all of creation. In John's Gospel, Jesus is the word made flesh, bread come down from heaven, the way, the life, the light, a vine, the good shepherd. His Christology is symbolic rather than prophetic, and his symbols for Christ help all Christians to articulate the

Christian vision in terms of everyday observable realities.

When the four Gospels are approached in this way, we are able to see how and why Christians can and should differ in their appreciation and understanding of Christian life. All four Gospels must eventually be integrated by each and every one of us, but the relative importance of any one Gospel will vary according to our life histories, the challenges of our environment and our perception of them.

From the four Gospels, we can then proceed to the letters and other books, such as Revelation. The letters will flesh out the implications of special questions in the domain of attitudes and behavior. In the case of Paul's letters, this is done from the point of view of Christ's death and resurrection. For Jesus, these came at the end and climax of his life. For us, however, Jesus' death and resurrection are events in the past and they give meaning to every facet of a life which strains forward to the day when we will join Christ in glory. The book of Revelation, on the other hand, looks most explicitly to the fulfillment of history and creation and examines our present life in light of them. All of life is drawn forth by Christian hope in the Lord's second coming. The book thus complements other works which emphasize rather how Christian life is propelled toward the future by the Lord's first coming.

By distinguishing four stages in the process of evangelization and by reflecting on how the New Testament either influences or is appropriately used at each stage, we avoid enormous frustration. We need not wonder why someone who has not yet met Christ and his Gospel remains unmoved by a Pauline argument, a Gospel synthesis or the New Testament as a whole.

The New Testament canon reflects the church's historical maturation. As a whole it meets the needs of a mature Christian who must face the challenges of personal and social ambiguity in Christian life (stage four). It presupposes a preliminary synthesis, in which the various dimensions of Christian living have been carefully interrelated within a hierarchy of values (stage three). This synthesis makes sense only if one has dealt with the various questions which arise from trying to live in a manner consistent with the Gospel (stage two). These questions, however, do not even arise, unless someone has first interiorized the very core of the Gospel as manifested in Jesus' person, death and resurrection (stage one). Without this initial grasp, all further efforts at evangelization are fruitless. However energetic and well-intentioned, they strike against ears which have not yet been opened to hear the Christian message.

Bibliographical Note

In order to acquire the attitude which is necessary for effective evangelization, few books are as effective as the Acts of the Apostles. Luke presents a church which is touched by the fire of Pentecost, which lives as a genuinely Christian community and which consequently proclaims its message with authority. Responding to internal crises and persecutions, that church extends its efforts to a widening audience until it reaches the very heart of the Roman empire. To appreciate Luke's achievement in Acts, Roberts J. Karris' *Invitation to Acts*, an Image Book (Garden City, New York: Doubleday & Company, Inc., 1978), Jerome Crowe's *The Acts in New Testament Message* (Wilmington: Michael Glazier, Inc., 1979), and my own *Acts of the Apostles,* published in the *Read and Pray* series (Chicago: Franciscan Herald Press, 1979) will prove helpful.

As in Luke's time, it is useful to read of the church's beginnings and its mission of evangelization. However, our task is considerably different from those beginnings, when the church was itself new. In the first century, primary evangelization led immediately to baptism. With the passing centuries, however, the church's own life and history became necessarily more complex as it assumed an increasingly more important position in human affairs. Baptism required a much longer preparation which climaxed in a final intensive "catechesis" for those who indicated their willingness to become Christians and to join the church.

A good example of such catecheses comes to us from St. Cyril of Jerusalem. We find it in *The Works of Saint Cyril of Jerusalem,* Vols. 1 and 2, translated by Leo P. McCauley and Anthony A. Stephenson, in *The Fathers of the Church,* Vols. 61 and 64 (Washington: The Catholic University of America Press, 1969, 1970). Together with a procatechesis or prologue, the first 18 of these classic lectures were delivered during Lent of 349 A.D. to catechumens who had requested to be baptized on Holy Saturday. They consequently presuppose initial or primary evangelization and must be situated along the stages of ongoing evangelization. In addition to these, Cyril delivered five lectures to the newly baptized, the mystagogical catecheses, during Easter Week. I shall refer to these in the chapter on the New Testament in catechesis.

In each of these lectures, Cyril comments on an important passage of scripture, usually drawn from the prophets or the Pauline letters. His effort is to show how these passages are related to the life on which his hearers wish to embark. In order to do this effectively, he draws from many related scripture texts and uses them to construct a synthesis on the subject presented.

The enormous amount of research and writing which is now appearing on the subject of adult development is especially significant for distinguishing evangelization into several stages. Among these, I would like to single out Erik H. Erikson's *Identity and the Life Cycle* (New York: W. W. Norton & Company, 1980). Erikson's personalist approach to human development makes this work, and his many other works, especially congenial for those who address life questions from a New Testament standpoint. His treatment of the way historical change affects ego identity helps us to appreciate the complexities of evangelization in a changing church which is involved in an even more rapidly changing world.

In *Christian Life Patterns* (Garden City, New York: Doubleday & Company, Inc., 1979), Evelyn Eaten Whitehead and James D. Whitehead discuss the psychological challenges and religious invitations of adult life. This book, which is about "adult religious growth for adults who are growing religiously" (p. 22), is especially sensitive to the Christian crises which Christians face in their development. It helps us to appreciate that the passage from one stage of evangelization to another, however complex, is essential for a healthy Christian and human life.

The spirit and energy which characterize evangelization can all too easily be dampened by the complexities of human psychological development, historical change and the church's insertion into the modern world. In an address which I gave at the 1978 conference of the Notre Dame Center for Pastoral Liturgy, I tried to show how the New Testament can help us to maintain or restore that spirit and energy. Entitled "Preaching the Call to Conversion," the address was published by National Catholic Reporter Cassettes (Kansas City, Mo., 1978) and condensed in the pages of *A.D. Correspondence,* Vol. 17, No. 3, July 29, 1978 (Notre Dame, Ind.: Ave Maria Press, 1978).

It is in the countries of the Third World that Paul VI's call to evangelization has been heard most clearly, and it is in those countries that the New Testament has been used most widely for purposes of evangelization. This work can be found primarily in the writings of the liberation theologians to whom I have referred in my introduction.

2
The New Testament in Catechesis

Catechesis is the most highly developed of church ministries and the one which, until recently, had the greatest influence on the life of the Christian community. In many countries, it long flourished in the context of Christian schools, where it became the dominant bearer of tradition and the source of Christian cohesiveness at the popular level. More recently, it burst the school's confines to focus on adults and assume its place as a ministry which accompanies Christians through every phase of their lives.

In our own times, other ministries such as evangelization and the various liturgical ministries have matured to a point where their rightful influence is equally pervasive. This development, however, has not displaced catechetics. On the contrary, it has sparked catechesis with new life. This is reflected in the shift of terminology from religious education to catechesis, and it has allowed catechesis to flower as one of several complementary ministries.

Supported by the Gospel's proclamation, catechesis has increasingly become what it should be, namely, reflection on the implications of a Gospel word which has been internalized. In partnership with the various stages of ongoing evangelization, catechesis enables Christians to understand the Gospel in relation to other areas of education for life.

Inspired by the renewed liturgy, catechesis enables

Christians to understand what they celebrate. In a vital collaboration with homiletics, it helps Christians to articulate and order the fundamental symbols which have always supported the church's life at levels which transcend full understanding and analysis. The church's sacramental self-expression thus grounds catechesis in the mystery of Christ. Without such grounding, catechesis becomes a mere education in one's religion and it gradually withers on a vine.

Catechesis is the first stage in the theological process through which faith gradually arrives at understanding. As a life effort which includes all Christians, it introduces a breadth of experience heretofore unknown into that process and provides much of the grist for the theological mill of specialists who devote their full attention to understanding the Christian mystery.

The scriptures, and in particular the New Testament, have provided much of the dynamism for the renewal of catechesis. Catechesis itself, following the development of biblical studies, has increasingly focused on the scriptures to the point where in our own day reflection on the scriptures has become a major component in catechetical ministry.

All too frequently, however, the catechist is satisfied with transferring the scientific discoveries and methodological processes which have been developed in biblical circles to the catechetical situation. Valuable as these may be, such a practice is inappropriate for catechesis, whose aim is not to popularize biblical scholarship and transform the Christian community into a host of biblical scholars.

To be effective, catechesis must employ methods of interpretation for communicating the biblical message and not those which are aimed at its objective understanding apart from the lives of those being catechized. They, of course, must arrive at understanding but at the kind of understanding which sees the New Testament as an expression of their own lives. From the catechist's point of view, the meaning of the New Testament must be derived from the communication process itself. He or she may be a biblical scholar. Catechesis, however, leads to an understanding which transcends that of biblical scholarship.

The scriptures have always held an important place in Christian education or catechesis. In modern times, following the extraordinary archeological and manuscript discoveries of the 19th and 20th centuries as well as the introduction of new historical and critical methods for studying the scriptures, the leadership of the church has repeatedly affirmed their place in Christian scholarship and education and granted them a prominence unprecedented since patristic and medieval times.

The official signal for this development was first sounded by Leo XIII in his encyclical letter *Providentissimus Deus* (Nov. 18, 1893), which was clearly a watershed in the church's attitude toward the scriptures and their study. Following Leo XIII's bold statement, each succeeding pontificate has addressed and promoted the study of scripture in Christian education or catechesis. Among the many statements, the encyclical letter of Pius XII, *Divino Afflante Spiritu* (Sept. 30, 1943) was particularly significant. To this day, it is recognized as the *magna carta* of Roman Catholic biblical studies, in that it encouraged Catholic biblical scholars to use modern methods of analysis and criticism. The work of Pius XII and his predecessors bore fruit in the Second Vatican Council's constitution

67

Dei Verbum (Word of God) (Nov. 18, 1965), which deals with divine revelation.

These achievements, however, were not without struggle. During the pontificate of St. Pius X, the church was faced with vast changes which radically affected its relationship to the world. The scriptures provided a means for situating the church in this changing world, but they did not spell out fixed limits for an authentic response. Confronted by a bewildering variety of views, many of which were threatening and some of which abandoned the very core of the church's unique identity and mission to the world, Pius X responded with a number of decrees which in fact stymied biblical studies until the publication of *Divino Afflante Spiritu.*

The pace of change continued to accelerate after the Second World War and the dismantling of the European colonial empires. The world moved into a new era, in which the secularization of life, especially in the West, became an enormous challenge. For some, this emerging social condition was welcomed as purifying and liberating for the church. Others reacted by reaffirming the church's traditional position *vis-a-vis* the world. Their struggle is reflected in the schemas which preceded the final text of various documents issued by Vatican II, including the constitution *Dei Verbum* and its courageous forward-looking statement on the nature of the scriptures and their relationship to revelation and church life.

Further struggles can be foreseen. In recent years, however, the scope of biblical studies has been enlarged. It is recognized that studies of the original context and intention of the scriptures are not adequate. We must refine our approach and examine the modern contexts in which the scriptures are read and to which they are applied. The present-day church and its place in the world are just as significant for understanding the scriptures as their original setting in life.

As in the past, our struggles reflect the seriousness with which the scriptures are received and the enormous repercussions they have on the shaping of church life. Ours is a world of interlocking relationships and dependencies in which the social, political and economic order is undergoing profound changes. In such a world and all its ambiguities, we cannot expect that all will perceive the church's role in the same way. As we face the future together, divergent views stemming from different vantage points must be expected and respected. As positions challenge and complement one another, the truth of the scriptures will appear for all who seek the way of Christ in continuity with the church's historical journey of nearly 2,000 years.

The above developments summarize the church's stance with regard to biblical studies in general and with special reference to those whose main concern is scholarly research. The scriptures, however, do not belong to the scholars, but to the church as such, a church repeatedly described by the Second Vatican Council in relation to the people of God. Accordingly, the scriptures belong to the entire Christian people, to all who are bonded in solidarity as the presence of Christ in the world. This realization is reflected in the explosion of biblical interest and study by thousands upon thousands who had once viewed these as the concern of church leaders and specialists.

Hungry for understanding, the people no longer allow their specialists to work in isolation, and these have responded to the church's need. In our times, biblical scholarship quickly moves into catechesis, and the latter helps to define and clarify the orientation of research.

For those, however, who are accustomed to equate the biblical word with their present understanding of it and who approach the scriptures as absolute and unchanging statements of God's word, this creates special difficulties. Developments in scholarship, from which they have a right to benefit, are treated either with suspicion or with the same reverence which they bring to the biblical word itself. The catechetical challenge seems obvious. As a church, we must work toward biblical literacy, a quality of understanding and wisdom which includes appreciation of the scriptures as they stood at our origins and as they formulate Christian life in our own times.

In general, literacy consists in the ability to read, that is, to interpret the accepted symbols and modes of written communication among human beings within a given culture. Since written language and its development are inseparable from a culture's literary heritage, literacy also includes a knowledge of one's literature.

The need for biblical literacy can be appreciated through a comparison with American literacy in English or in the language associated with any other major cultural strain in the modern world. To understand life and communication in the United States, all who are either born in our country or who migrate to it study the literature which expressed and shaped our vision, attitudes and ways of doing. The alternative is to remain a foreigner, isolated from the dominant culture. The process begins with the rudiments of the English language as it has developed on our shores. It soon turns to the literature, and the student of English becomes familiar with the various contexts in which the language has been and continues to be used. Sensitive to the evocative power of words and phrases, the student gradually becomes at home in English. Not everyone, of course, becomes equally literate, but a high degree of literacy remains the ideal for all.

If we take literacy in the secular realm so seriously, ought we not to have similar expectations in the religious realm? Every aspect of our religious life is affected by the language which shapes us as a Christian people, and that language is indissolubly bound to the scriptures, the classical literature of God's word to Christians. Taking our Christian life as seriously as our secular life, the scriptures should be given a prominent place in our catechesis. The alternative is to remain foreigners, outsiders who profess Christian faith but are never quite at home with it. Without biblical literacy, Christian life becomes marginalized, unintegrated in life as a whole, condemned to the periphery of the core values which orient life and constitute our culture.

The various magisterial statements to which I have referred provide the stimulus and the encouragement to move toward biblical literacy on a broad scale. Such an effort, however, must be integrated in the more general catechetical ministry. The main lines for this ministry were spelled out in the General Catechetical Directory which Pope Paul VI approved on March 18, 1971. This directory was developed and applied in *Sharing the Light of Faith*, the national catechetical directory for Catholics of the United States.

Equally important for catechesis is the apostolic exhortation of Pope John Paul II on catechetics, *Catechesi Tradendae* (Oct. 16, 1979). Like *Evangelii Nuntiandi*, this exhortation reflects the mind of a general assembly of the synod of bishops (Oct. 1977). Part of Paul VI's

71

unfinished agenda, the task of writing the exhortation passed to John Paul I and subsequently to John Paul II. It can be found in *Origins* (Nov. 8, 1979) 9:329, 331-347.

The Witness of the New Testament

The witness of the New Testament for catechesis is manifold. The following pages will concentrate on two areas of special concern, that of biblical literacy in the New Testament period and the Gospels' presentation of the teacher-disciple relationship which characterized the life of Jesus and his first followers.

Biblical Literacy   The Christians of New Testament times were biblically literate. This is obvious from the New Testament itself, where nearly every work relies very heavily on the Old Testament scriptures for understanding and for presenting Christian realities and challenges. As in modern life, however, such literacy admitted of degrees. At one pole we have the Epistle to the Hebrews, which is extremely sophisticated in its use of scripture. At the other, we have the pastoral epistles, that is, 1 and 2 Timothy and Titus, which speak of the scriptures but use them very little.

In view of the central role which the scriptures played in Jewish life, it comes as no surprise that Jesus and the earliest Christians, who were of Jewish origin, would have known the scriptures so well and would have been at home in their interpretation. The scriptures functioned as the cornerstone of Jewish popular education. The scrolls presented the Law as the accepted norm of life and prosperity in a world created and ruled by

72

God. There were also the prophets, who had repeatedly called the people to fidelity in the course of a troubled history. In addition, there were the psalms, timeless hymns and prayers for communal and personal worship. Finally, there were scrolls of wisdom, indicating how a good Israelite was to live and act in the concrete circumstances of life and according to each one's social responsibilities.

It is truly amazing, however, that the Gentile Christians, who soon dominated the life of the church and who had been foreign to the biblical world of first-century Judaism, were also biblically literate. Mark's Gospel, a synthesis of the Christian message for a community of Gentiles, found it necessary to explain contemporary Jewish customs. However, no such explanation was needed for its use of the scriptures, whose language and literary forms permeate the entire text. The same is true of Luke, who demonstrated extraordinary subtlety and astuteness in the use of scripture. Like Mark, Luke presupposes that Gentile readers are comfortable and familiar with the scriptures themselves as well as with the traditional modes of interpretation. Paul's letters, whose readers included many Gentiles, also provide an important witness. In some churches, such as that of Rome, Gentiles actually predominated at the time of Paul's writing. Yet, his letter to the Romans is thoroughly dependent on the scriptures, and without a good grasp of the Old Testament, the letter would have been altogether unintelligible.

In the early Pauline mission, the Gentiles were men and women who had been associated with the synagogue and who had participated in its biblical educative process. Familiarity with the scriptures thus stemmed from their pre-Christian past. Within a short time, however, the main source of Gentile adherents to the Gospel was no longer the synagogue but every conceivable point of social communication in the Hellenistic cities of the time. Gentiles who turned to Christianity must consequently have received a gradual but profound grounding in the scriptures. From the general usage of the Jewish scriptures in New Testament writings, we can assume that this did not require the learning of Semitic languages. The Septuagint, a Greek translation effected at Alexandria, had already spread throughout the world of Hellenistic Judaism and it had become the Bible of the New Testament Christians.

In our times, it is difficult to imagine that Gentiles, foreigners to biblical culture, would have been so successful at integrating the scriptures into their culture. We ourselves frequently find the biblical world so remote that the task appears overwhelming and we wonder at the very possibility of doing this intelligently on a popular scale. Yet, the fact remains that, although Jewish customs and sabbath observance were set aside, the scriptures remained a key element in Gentile Christian life. In this matter, we stand challenged by the practice and achievement of early Gentile Christianity, for which the scriptures were an indispensable element in Christian literacy.

The Hellenistic world did possess an advantage which we do not have. Young Hellenes were educated in works which were somewhat analogous to the scriptures. Homer's epics, long associated with the origins of their civilization, provided the basis of education, and all who were born in that civilization or came to it from the outside were taught through their poems of gods, heroes, cities, battles and journeys. Since these works belonged to another age and to a more limited Aegean environment, they had to be interpreted. The modes of interpretation or hermeneutics which developed in the schools had already been applied to the scriptures, especially at Alexandria.

Hellenistic Gentiles, for whom Homer represented writings comparable to the biblical canon, found it considerably easier to replace Homer with Moses than it is for us to take up Moses in a world which has no Homer or his equivalent. Lack of a congenial reference point such as Homer, however, does not excuse us from taking on the challenge of biblical literacy. The lines which have been drawn between religion and the secular in modern life and education can also work to our advantage. For Hellenes, the Homeric text had a quasi-sacred quality, imbuing its position in life with a strong resistance to change. For us, the Gentiles of the modern world, for whom the Old and New Testament religious environments appear extremely remote, the scriptures can respond to the religious vacuum of secular education. The critical issue is consequently not so much our remoteness from the ancient cultures but whether we actually do share in the same faith experience which found its classical expression in the scriptures.

Jesus as Catechist   The Gospels present Jesus as a proclaimer, healer, exorcist and reconciler. All of these functions correspond to his life status and historical mission as an itinerant prophet, and they no doubt constitute a good description of what his life in fact was all about. In faith, Christians would gradually come to recognize that the prophet whom they had known and responded to was more than a prophet. He was the Christ, the Lord, the Son of Man and the Son of God.

The Christians for their part stood in continuity with Jesus' first followers as they too followed him on a way which passed through suffering and the passion to a glorious life with God.

The Gospels, however, also presented Jesus as a teacher, as one who interpreted the Law and the prophets for a new age and for specific situations in history. As a teacher, Jesus also plumbed the depths and revealed the heights of Israel's wisdom, and he further developed that wisdom to enable his hearers to discern what it meant to follow him and what this required in light of various social roles and responsibilities.

Unlike Jesus' other functions, that of teacher corresponds somewhat less to his mission as an itinerant prophet. The first-century Jewish teacher could be an itinerant, but he normally remained in one place, at least for a long period of time, and he taught in the context of a synagogue. In his capacity as teacher, Jesus was called Rabbi or Master, and his followers were referred to as disciples. In faith, the disciples would eventually recognize that their teacher was divine and that his message constituted a new revelation of God's word.

Teaching does indeed appear to have been one of Jesus' historical activities. However, there can be little doubt that the Gospels extended the scope of his teaching and gave it a place in his life which far exceeded what in fact had been the case. In the Gospels, all of Jesus' functions, including Gospel proclamation, healing, exorcising and reconciling are referred to as teaching.

This development stems from two closely related sources. First, early Christianity had moved from its initial stage as a reform movement to a situation in which local communities had emerged as focal points for both life and mission. Second, these local communities, which were analogous to synagogues, required the ministerial attention of teachers or catechists who enabled them to develop as genuinely Christian in the urban world of the Roman empire. These catechists adapted the work and message of Jesus, which had been intended primarily for men and women who were not yet followers, to this new situation. Thus it is that the Gospels present Jesus primarily as a teacher and his followers as disciples learning at the feet of the master.

A good example of how Jesus' other activities have been transformed into teaching ministry can be found in Mark 1:21-28. The heart of this passage lies in an encounter between Jesus and a man with an unclean spirit. Defiantly challenged by the demons who speak through the man, Jesus rebukes the unclean spirit and successfully orders him out of the man (1:23-26). This event is situated in the Capernaum synagogue where Jesus was teaching with authority, as the author says, and not like the scribes (1:21-22). The assembly's reaction to the exorcism is that Jesus' command and the obedience of the unclean spirits is a new teaching (1:27-28).

Jesus' action (1:23-26) had led to a story which became useful for Christian catechesis. In itself, however, it was an exorcism. It may well have taken place, as the text indicates, while Jesus was teaching (1:21-22), but it is only in the Gospel tradition that the exorcism event came to be seen as Jesus' teaching (1:27-28). For Jesus and the account's earliest telling, it may have demonstrated the authority with which Jesus taught as well as the ultimate purpose of his teaching, namely the overcoming of the demonic in Jesus' hearers, but the exorcism was not formally a teaching act.

As a teacher, Jesus was known for his wisdom sayings, and these can be found throughout the accounts of his ministry. Many have also been gathered into discourses, syntheses of Jesus' teaching concerning major aspects of Christian living and history. Among these, the best known are the five great discourses presented in Matthew (Mt 5-7; 10; 13; 18; 23-25). The first of these discourses, which is popularly called Jesus' Sermon on the Mount, includes the beatitudes (5:3-10), the reinterpretation of the law of Moses (5:17-48), sayings on fasting, prayer and giving alms (6:1, 2-4, 5-6, 16-18) and many others.

The Gospels are careful to situate Jesus' sayings in concrete life settings. So anchored, the sayings cannot be divorced from life's many challenges. They never become absolute statements of a divine revelation which would allow Christians to perceive their challenge purely in terms of an escape to the otherworldly. Even the discourses, which witness to the universality of Jesus' sayings, are presented as part of Jesus' Gospel story and not as complete Gospels in themselves.

It is in the parables, however, that we encounter Jesus the teacher at his best. These parables reveal the meaning of Jesus' sayings and show how they are to be understood concretely by illustrating their implications in story form. Luke's beatitude concerning the poor (you poor) who have the kingdom of God (6:20) and his parallel woe concerning the rich (you rich) who have received their consolation (6:24) is marvelously illustrated by his parable of the rich man and poor Lazarus whose conditions are ultimately reversed (16:19-31). Such parables, with whose personages the reader can identify, clothe Jesus' sayings with flesh and blood. They drive the saying to the very heart and mind of the hearer or reader, who experiences its message as a dynamic personal drama with all the feelings, fears and hopes which make up human life.

Many of the parables deal with nature, with the planting of seeds, the growth of a crop, the admixture of weeds and the harvest, with other things that grow like the lilies of the field and the mustard bush, with the seasons, such as spring, and with all those things which are experienced in daily life. They tell of lamps and their lampstands, loaves and their leaven, weddings and garments. Never remote from the experience of Jesus' hearers, the parables draw out the significance of simple things. We betray the teaching potential of Jesus' parables when we reduce them to a single point or abstract ethical principle. The parables communicated rather by presenting a complex of elements which mirrored the life of Jesus' hearers and they placed these in their relationships.

In their original context, Jesus' parables were absolutely lucid. This does not mean that their meaning was closed and that the people felt satisfied when they came to their conclusion. Having learned the parable, listeners would thus have moved on to something else and the parable's vitality as an agent in Christian catechesis would have ended. On the contrary, the parables challenged all who had ears to hear Jesus' intent and moved them to pursue an endless process of reflection. Leaving Jesus' company, the people bore the parable with them and mulled over what it required of them in various life situations and in the multiplicity of their relationships and challenges.

As Christian history and life moved on, however, the parables frequently lost their lucidity and impact. They were thus retold and allegorically reinterpreted in the community of disciples. Such is the process which underlies Mark 4:1-20. Jesus' parable of the sower (4:3-9) had become opaque (4:10-13) for Christians living in a new age. Christian tradition and the Markan author set out to interpret it in light of the disciples' preaching experience (4:14-20), and the parable of the sower thus remained a vital challenging story in the Christian community.

Mark 4:1-20 includes both Jesus' parable and the community's allegorical application. In so doing it leaves us a model of how the Christians of our own time may anchor themselves in Jesus' parable teaching even as they reinterpret it for a new moment of history.

Our brief synthesis of catechesis in the New Testament showed how the early Christians took up the challenge of biblical literacy even in Gentile Christianity where the Old Testament scriptures were foreign and unfamiliar. It also examined Jesus' mission as a teacher and how Christian tradition came to see all of Jesus' work as catechesis. In doing this, the Christians drew out the meaning of Jesus' sayings and parables for their own developing context and situated Jesus' teaching within the story of his whole life. This synthesis will guide our steps as we take up the use of New Testament stories in modern catechesis and present a mode of interpretation which should facilitate their reading in the teaching ministry.

Teaching the New Testament's Gospel

As a teacher, Jesus employed the various teaching modes prevalent in first-century Palestinian Judaism. The early Christians did the same, but as the context of Christianity extended across the eastern and central provinces of the empire, they also turned to the teaching methods current in the Hellenistic world outside of Judaism. Some of these methods coincided with those of Judaism. Among these, the most significant consisted in storytelling.

Jesus himself had been an extremely gifted storyteller. Learning from him and from one another, his followers developed similar skills. The Gospels and the Acts of the Apostles present some of the finest examples of their art. In the New Testament, however, the basic oral form of storytelling has been transformed into writing.

Jesus' stories were told and heard. The New Testament's stories are meant to be read. However, since reading in early times was frequently done aloud and for the benefit of others, it too was meant to be heard. As such, the New Testament stories remain close to living oral communication, but they also share in the basic form, structure and technique of literature.

The fact that New Testament stories are meant to be read aloud and heard defines the nature of our task as we explore how we can teach the New Testament Gospel. My purpose is to contribute first to the development of good Christian storytellers, to men and women who can take a written Gospel story and read it aloud so that its communicative potential springs to life. Second, I aim to help those who read the story for themselves or hear it from others to discern what is significant in the story.

To achieve these goals, we must become sensitive to the elements which enter into a story as well as to the way they are combined to make the story what it is. As in a recipe, it is not enough to know the ingredients. We must also know how they are joined to produce the final

81

result. The task is consequently one of analysis and of synthesis in which the two proceed hand in hand.

The elements of a story correspond to a set of basic questions: Where? When? Who? What? How? Why? When we answer these questions carefully, the various elements of the story come into focus. When we follow the given order in answering them, the story gradually takes shape. Beginning with the simplest elements, we move toward the more complex and arrive at a good appreciation of the full story in all its interrelationships. The better to achieve this, a second set of basic questions is interwoven into the first. For example, after establishing the story's spatial (Where?) and temporal (When?) cadre, we immediately ask: Where-When? Over and above the two elements involved, the very combination might prove significant. Later we ask Where-When-Who?; and so forth.

In the following pages, we shall explore the meaning of the questions which we bring to a story in relation, first, to a variety of New Testament stories and, second, in relation to a single story (Lk 10:38-42). The process we shall outline produces the best results when it is employed as a group effort in which the participants share their observations and help one another to discern what is truly in the story.

The Questions

Where? Where does the action or event take place? The question refers to elements of geography and physical location. For example, an event might occur at the Jordan River as in the case of Jesus' baptism. But does the Spirit's descent take place as Jesus emerges from the water (Mk 1:10) or later while Jesus is at prayer (Lk 3:21)? Does the event take place at the temple (Lk 2:27), in a synagogue (Lk 6:6), in a home (Lk 7:36), beside a road (Mk 10:46) or on a road (Lk 24:13, 35)? Is it next to a lake, as in Mark 4:1-34? But then is everyone beside the lake or is Jesus in a boat on the water as he instructs the crowd on the shore (Mk 4:1)? Does the event transfer from one place to another as from a customs post to a reception hall in somone's house (Lk 5:27-32)? If no place is indicated, the story could be situated anywhere, and the event acquires a certain spatial universality

As the inquiry proceeds, such questions may become extremely significant from a theological point of view. For the moment, however, one should not jump to conclusions which are unwarranted by the observations. It suffices that the setting be clearly visualized and that the imagination be fully engaged. Further reflection on the passage and the Gospel as a whole will continue to build on foundations which have been laid with care.

When? When does the action or event take place? This question is intimately related to the first, and it could actually have been asked before the question of location. Together, the two questions provide the basic coordinates of space and time within which any story develops. In theater, they correspond to the stage, the set and the lighting, which combine to define both space and time.

Does the incident take place in the morning, just after sunrise (Mk 16:1), while it was still dark (Jn 20:1), or at the three o'clock hour of prayer (Acts 3:1)? Does it occur on a feast (Lk 2:41), as a feast is approaching (Lk 22:1), or on a sabbath (Lk 6:1, 6)? Is the time given in relation to a prior event (Lk 7:1)? Does it proceed from one moment to another, as from the feast of Passover to the third day (Lk 2:41-42, 46) or from some point during the night to cockcrow (Lk 22:54-62)? Perhaps no time is specified. In this case, the story could occur anytime, and it acquires a certain temporal universality.

As with the question concerning location, the answer to this second question might eventually contribute to the story's theological and pastoral significance. For the moment, however, it is best not to move too hastily to conclusions. It suffices to clothe the place which has been visualized with a sense of time, with light, darkness, the heat of day or the heightened feelings which surround a feast.

Where-When? At times, the conjunction of place and time is itself significant. For example, is a journey to Jerusalem related to the feast of Passover (Lk 2:41-52)? Is Jesus in a synagogue on the sabbath (Lk 6:6)? Is someone going to the temple at the hour of prayer (Acts 3:1)? After asking the questions of place and time, we must consequently approach the two questions together. In this way, the discreet data begin to combine into a preliminary synthesis, and the story as such begins to take shape.

Who? Who are the personages involved in the story? This question is more difficult than the previous questions. It must be answered in two distinct phases.

First, we must carefully list all the participants, a deceptively simple task. As when people enter a room or a crowd, the tendency is to focus on several of the personages and not to note the presence of others. Our interests and expectations must not be allowed to filter out some of the participants from the story. Those we pass over may play a very significant role. In Jesus' parable of the prodigal son, for example, the personages include the father, the younger son, the older son, servants and those who were called to the celebration banquet (Lk 15:11-32). In Matthew's account of the cure of a paralytic, the personages are Jesus, the people, the paralytic, some of the scribes and the crowd (Mt 9:1-8).

In this same phase, we must note how the personages are introduced and described. In the story of Jesus and Zacchaeus, the latter is first named and then presented as the chief tax collector in Jericho and a wealthy man. He is also described as small of stature (Lk 19:2). Jesus, on the other hand, is not described. He is referred to by his name Jesus (Lk 19:3, 5, 9) as well as by two titles, Lord (Lk 19:8) and the Son of Man (Lk 19:10).

In the second phase, we must ask who is presented as the principal personage. In the Gospels, Jesus is the principal personage in nearly every story which he does not himself tell. Our question, however, must usually prescind from this general role and concern the principal personage among those who make this particular story distinctive. In Luke's account of the call of the first disciples (5:1-11), the personages include Jesus, the crowd, the fishermen, Simon, his shipmates, and his partners, James and John. Among these, Simon is the principal personage. Singled out from the crowds and the fishermen, he is the owner of the boat in which Jesus embarks. He accompanies Jesus in the boat, and Jesus speaks to him apart from the crowds. Simon is also the only one who participates in the dialogue. Besides, the shipmates and the partners are introduced in relation to him and not vice versa. They are described as his shipmates and his partners. Were the members of one of these groups central, Simon would be presented as their shipmate or their partner.

After identifying the principal personage, we must note how he or she is positioned with regard to Jesus and the other participants. Zacchaeus, for example, is above the crowd in a sycamore (Lk 19:4), and he looks down as Jesus looks up to him (Lk 19:5). This is an important moment of contact. He then descends and stands in the midst of the crowd. It is in that situation that Jesus engages him in dialogue (Lk 19:6-10). To appreciate what is said, we must be mindful of Zacchaeus' relationship to the crowd. Another good example is Mark's account of the sequel to Peter's confession (Mk 8:31-33). While addressing Peter, Jesus does not look at him but at the disciples (Mk 8:33). The implication is that Jesus' concern is not only with Peter but with the disciples whom Peter is tempting.

Where-When-Who? Now that we have identified the personages, noted how they are described, distinguished the principal one, and positioned them with regard to one another, we must inquire into their special significance, if any, with regard to place and time. Zechariah, for example, is a priest and not an ordinary Jew (Lk 1:5). When the angel appears to him to announce the conception of John the Baptist, he is fulfilling his official priestly functions in the temple (Lk 1:8). In Acts 12:12, when Peter escapes from prison, he goes to the house of Mary, the mother of John whose other name was Mark. The house of Mary was a place of assembly for the early Christian community. A woman is thus presented as the hostess for a "house-church." As we answer the comprehensive question

Where-When-Who?, we continue to draw the elements of the story into the emerging synthesis begun with Where-When?

What? With the first three questions, we focused on all the static elements of the story. We introduced the physical coordinates of space and time, and we situated the personages within these and with regard to one another. We also noted the different successive moments in the story, in which the scene changes, personages are repositioned, and new personages may be introduced. Our observations at this point may be compared to staging plans or slides taken at different moments in a play. A succession of these may suggest change and movement, but in themselves they are stills.

Our next question concerns the story's movement. It deals with what happens in the story. With it, our stage comes to life and its *dramatis personae* begin to act, to interrelate and to speak to one another. In the process, we recognize that an attitude or sets of attitudes are set forth, challenged and altered.

Jesus' story of the good Samaritan (Lk 10:30-35), for example, is part of a larger story concerning Jesus and a lawyer (Lk 10:25-37). In this story, the lawyer asks what he must do to inherit everlasting life, and Jesus leads him to unveil a significant aspect of his attitude, which is problematic. The lawyer knows what he must do, but then he would like to distinguish between those who are his neighbor and those who are not. He would thus be able to limit the application of the commandment which calls for love of one's neighbor (Lk 10:25-29).

In his response, Jesus tells the story of a good Samaritan and shows how the real neighbor might well be the person whom the lawyer would exclude (Lk 10:30-35). He then draws this very response from the lawyer. However, Jesus' concluding statement resituates the entire issue. The responsibility for qualifying as neighbor must not be placed on others. Rather, it is the lawyer's responsibility to be a good neighbor to others (Lk 10:36-37). The story has thus substituted the question which should have been asked for the one which the lawyer had brought to Jesus. The critical question is not who is my neighbor (Lk 10:29), but how can I be a neighbor to others (Lk 10:37b). The one who is a true neighbor to others (Lk 10:27) without distinction (Lk 10:36-37a) is the one who inherits everlasting life (Lk 10:25).

From the above story, it becomes obvious that our question concerns the problem which is taken up and confronted in the story. To answer this question, however, one must be able to distinguish various points of view. The question, what is the problem, cannot be answered unless we add, from whose point of view.

In the story of Jesus and the lawyer, this was simple, since the story includes only two personages. Our observations had only to distinguish the lawyer's point of view from that of Jesus. However, when the story includes many personages, it is essential that we have identified the principal personage. Having done so, we then ask what the problem is from his or her point of view.

In a Lukan story of repentance and forgiveness (Lk 7:36-50), the *dramatis personae* include Jesus, a Pharisee named Simon, a woman who was publicly known as a sinner, and Jesus' fellow guests. The principal personage is Simon the Pharisee, a fact which may be obscured by modern biblical editors, who tend to entitle this story "The Penitent Woman." Jesus is dining in the home of the Pharisee who had invited him (Lk 7:36) and, save for 7:48-50, the entire dialogue takes place between Jesus and this Pharisee.

From the Pharisee's point of view, the problem is threefold. The sinful woman has touched Jesus. Jesus has allowed her to do so without reproach. His behavior is not compatible with the prophetic role. The Pharisee's implied conclusion is that Jesus must not be a prophet (Lk 7:39).

From Jesus' point of view, the problem lies in the Pharisee's attitude toward the woman, his presuppositions concerning the role of a prophet and his assumption concerning what Jesus should do. Beginning with a parable, Jesus shows that the woman's love called for Jesus' forgiving response to her. Her great love led to the forgiveness of her many sins. As one who loves little, the Pharisee himself is forgiven little. He had not seen that the woman came to Jesus out of love, and that this love called for forgiveness. The Pharisee's own love was little, and therein lay the real problem (Lk 7:40-48).

Jesus' fellow guests extend one aspect of the Pharisee's appreciation of the problem, that of Jesus' identity: "Who is this, who even forgives sins?" (Lk 7:49). Jesus, however, focuses their attention away from his identity to the woman's faith. It is her faith which saved her. Recognizing her faith, Jesus sent her in peace (Lk 7:50). The guests should attend to their own faith rather than to Jesus' identity.

In the story, the woman has no problem whatsoever. She came to Jesus with the needed love and faith, and she was duly forgiven and sent forth in peace. Her role was simply to draw out the problems of the principal personage and of the supporting actors and to provide an occasion for Jesus' response to these.

Where-When-Who-What? After examining the story's basic theme or problem, we once again attend to the emerging synthesis. The problem may be related precisely to a place and time in which the principal personage and the others in the story have a specific role and responsibility. For example, in a Lukan event (Lk 9:12-17) which follows the return of the apostles from a mission (time), the twelve (principal personages) come to Jesus when the day begins to wear away (time). The event is situated in a city called Bethsaida, where crowds have followed Jesus (place). From the point of view of the twelve, it is necessary to send the crowds away to find food and lodging for themselves (Lk 9:12). They do not wish to assume a responsibility which appears overwhelming and impossible to fulfill (Lk 9:13b-14a). From Jesus' point of view, the twelve must assume this responsibility and they are capable of nourishing the crowds (Lk 9:13a, 14b-17) whom Jesus has welcomed, taught and healed (Lk 9:11).

How? In our examination of the story's spatial and temporal coordinates, personages and movement, we attended to what the story says. We now alter our perspective and examine the story as a reality in itself. How is the story told? What role does the narrator play? How does dialogue or a discourse contribute to the story? How are names, titles, special terms and language in general used? The answers to such questions will greatly extend our grasp of the story's theological and pastoral import.

First, we must explore the role of the narrator, who

provides the story with order and clarity. It is generally he who provides the introduction, transitions and conclusion. In the story of Emmaus, for example (Lk 24:13-35), he is entirely reponsible for 24:13-16 (the introduction), for major elements in 24:28-29 (a transition) for much of 24:31-35 (the conclusion). It is he who indicates which personage is speaking (24:17a, 18a, 19a, 25a, 29a, 32a, 33b), who summarizes most of Jesus' discourse (25:27), describes the meal event (24:30), and summarizes the two disciples' report concerning what happened to them (24:35). In this last summary, he distinguishes the event's two phases, what happened on the road (24:17-27) and how they came to know him in the breaking of bread (24:30). These two phases had been joined by the transition in 24:28-29, and he had framed all of 24:17-30 between two verses concerning the disciples' non-recognition and their recognition of who Jesus was (24:16, 31).

In theater, all of these functions are usually unnecessary, since the audience sees and hears everything that occurs. We need not be told, for example, who is speaking. We both see and hear the actor or actress do so. The role which best corresponds to the narrator is that of the director who planned the play's unfolding according to the playwright's indications. When the curtain parts, his role is finished and he has already disappeared. In a written story, on the other hand, the narrator remains on the scene to direct the action as it unfolds.

The narrator provides the reader with everything required to follow the story. As we have indicated, he may be compared to the director of a play. His function, however, frequently transcends that of the director. Taking advantage of the story's literary medium, he can provide the readers with information which the personages in the story do not have. In the story of Emmaus, for example, the narrator tells us that the person whom the two disciples have been prevented from recognizing is Jesus himself. Privy to this special information, the readers empathize with the disciples and experience their disillusionment, but they also distance themselves from the disciples and share the stance of the narrator. This dual stance is important for the story's pastoral effectiveness in shaping the Christian reader's attitude. Throughout the story, we are made to confront what seems to be with what actually is. The same technique is employed when the narrator tells us that Jesus acted as if he were going farther (24:28). Unlike the disciples, we know that Jesus has no intention of going farther. The disciples' stance and that of the narrator combine to generate a tension within the reader, and this tension is finally resolved at the moment of recognition, when we join the disciples in celebrating, refining our understanding and sharing our discovery.

In relation to theater, this all-knowing and confiding function of the narrator may be compared to that of the chorus in classical Greek drama or to Milton's role in Penderecki's recent opera *Paradise Lost*.

Dialogue clearly enhances a story's liveliness. This, however, is the least of its functions. When the narrator quotes personages, he may allow attitudes and points of view other than his own to speak out in the story. He may also introduce statements from Jesus the risen Lord, from a heavenly voice or from angels, all of which transcend the limitations of his own person.

With dialogue, the narrator steps aside and allows personages to interact. No longer does he communicate directly but through the combined effect of the personages' interaction as statements, pronouncements and challenges are made, questions asked and responded to, exclamations uttered and commands or warnings given.

The fact that the narrator controls the dialogue allows for considerable subtlety. In the story of Emmaus, for example, Jesus' role in the early part of the dialogue (24:17-19a) is aimed at drawing out the two disciples, who then express their view of the situation (24:19b-24). Only then is Jesus able to respond to them concretely (24:25-26).

The disciples' statements, on the other hand, are full of irony. As they ask Jesus if he is only one who does not know what has recently occurred in Jerusalem (24:18), the reader already knows Jesus' identity and that he had been at the very center of the drama. In their response to Jesus, they outline Jesus' story from the vantage point of their discouragement. In doing so, however, they use many of the classic expressions of Christian faith and hope. Jesus is a prophet, powerful in word and deed before God and all the people. He was delivered up by the chief priests and leaders. Their expectations that he would set Israel free have been shattered. Now it is the third day and those who went to the tomb failed to see Jesus (24:19b-24). The reader, however, knows that Jesus showed himself the powerful prophet and the savior of Israel precisely in the act of being delivered up, that the third day is that of his manifestation as risen Lord, and that the unrecognizing disciples are even now seeing him.

From the above observations on the narrator's control over dialogue, it is obvious that the use of language is very significant. Readers, however, should take notice of a few additional factors. Does the narrator draw language from a well-known context? Does he refer to a biblical term or expression? In Luke 9:31, for example, the narrator states that Moses and Elijah spoke with Jesus of his coming "exodus," a term which evokes Israel's departure from Egypt and servitude. Does he use a liturgical expression as in the multiplication of loaves, a story of marvelous sharing, when Jesus takes the loaves, gives thanks, breaks them and gives them to his disciples to distribute (Mk 6:41; 8:6)? Such usage assimilates the story to the liturgical context of the early Christians.

How does the narrator use titles? If Jesus is presented as Lord, as in Luke 11:1, the narrative views the event as part of the historical life of Jesus as well as of the community's post-resurrection context. This historical life is actually rearticulated with regard to the post-resurrection context. Now that Jesus is risen, it does not suffice to speak of Jesus' prayer. Since the community continues to be taught by the Lord's presence, one must speak of the Lord's prayer. Finally, one must pay attention to the significance of the groups identified. In Luke, for example, the Pharisees evoke a major category of actors in Jesus' story, but the way they are treated indicates that they also refer to Christians who have adopted the same stance. In modern parlance, we would refer to them as neo-Pharisees or Christian "Pharisees."

Where-When-Who-What-How? Before proceeding to our last questions, we must once again attend to our developing synthesis. The task is now to see the relationship between the story's formal elements, that is, how it is told, and its material elements, namely, its physical and temporal setting, its personages and their interchange or movement. It is at this point that we move beyond what the story is about and come to grips with its potential to communicate. The story as such has an intention which transcends the event to which it refers and which addresses the event to the readers. This intentionality dominates and conditions what is told, accounts for the selection of what is included and how the elements are presented.

In ordinary life, the difference between an event and the way it is communicated is clearly sensed, and we quite naturally take it into consideration. We sense it, for example, when we speak of a family tragedy and adapt our telling of it to parents or to children. In each case, we shape the story so that it will communicate most effectively with those to whom we tell it. We take their background, attitudes and perceptions into consideration, and the latter have much to do with the way we share the event. Aware that the event's significance varies for different listeners, we instinctively adapt our telling of it to specific situations.

What is true of daily life applies to stories in the New Testament. For example, the story of the multiplication of loaves refers to an event in Jesus' life. However, it is told in such a way that the meaning of the event will be clear to the people addressed. In all six accounts of this event (Mk 6:34-44; 8:1-9; Mt 14:13-21; 15:32-38; Lk 9:10-17; Jn 6:1-13) the Gospel writers want the readers to see how the event is related to their celebration of the Lord's Supper. Accordingly, all describe Jesus' action with language drawn from early liturgical texts which were used in the weekly assembly: Jesus took bread, blessed or gave thanks, broke it and gave it to the disciples. In the synoptic Gospels, we also note that Jesus does not personally give the bread to the people but that he gives it to the disciples or to the twelve to distribute. This additional adaptation to the context of the early communities is related to the texts' emphasis on the abundance of bread left over for future meals.

The marvelous sharing which was inspired and mediated by Jesus was also told in a manner which respected distinct persons addressed. In Mark 6:34-44, we have a traditional account intended for Jewish Christians. In Mark 8:1-9, this account is supplemented by a Gentile Christian tradition which bears on the same event. Luke, who wrote for Gentile Christians living in the major cities of the eastern Roman Empire, situated the event in the urban milieu of Bethsaida rather than in the desert or countryside (Lk 9:10-17). In his account, the crowd does not sit on the ground or on green grass but at tables according to the established practice for the breaking of bread.

Why? After exploring what the story says (Where? When? Who? What?) and how it is told (How?), we now move from the story as a reality in itself to its pastoral relationship to the readers. Why does the author share this story with the readers? Something in the life of the community must call for this story.

A basic assumption in all storytelling is that the story is of interest to the readers. To be of interest, it must somehow be their story as well as that of the storyteller. When this is true, the story is a good one. It is remembered and repeated. When this is not true, it is a bad one and soon forgotten. When the story applies to a larger audience than that which was originally intended, it reaches beyond the original audience and acquires a larger one of its own. When the audience proves to be universal in any particular time and across all barriers of time, the story is deemed classical. Such are the stories in the Gospels and Acts.

As with some of our previous questions, the story's "why" includes two phases. In the first, we reflect on the original audience as perceived by the author and revealed in the narrative. In the second, we reflect on our own contemporary audience and ask how the story relates to Christians in the modern world. Both phases require delicate attention to the story and its unfolding. Since the New Testament stories are Christian classics, whose universality coincides with that of the church, we must take special care not to limit their applicability to what we presently perceive through our limited individual experience of life realities and Christian values. In examining the "why" of the story, we must consequently maintain a sense of open-endedness. As we ourselves develop, the story is bound to become more meaningful.

The Gospels' emphasis on Judas' betrayal in the accounts of the Last Supper provides a good example. Why does the Gospel writer dwell so extensively on the betrayal? Why does he not focus on other personages and on other events rather than on something which appears so negative? Within the story, the betrayal provides an important and necessary link with the whole passion story in which the Last Supper is situated. The passion, however, leads to the resurrection, and it would have been possible to deemphasize the betrayal in favor of Jesus' own gift of himself, a gift which God accepted and to which he responded with the resurrection or exaltation. And yet, the betrayal is clearly emphasized.

It must be that the Gospel writers were aware of betrayals in the life of the Christian community. For the story of the Last Supper to be the community's story, the betrayal consequently had to be included. Without it, the account would have been pastorally inadequate. Judas' betrayal was indeed a historical fact, but it is not told for its own sake. Many other historical facts were passed over and not relevant to the intended audience.

In Luke's Gospel, Jesus' statement concerning the betrayer (22:21-22) leads to a dispute as to which of those present would do such a deed (22:23). The answer is given in the following verse (22:24), which speaks of a new dispute concerning who should be regarded as the greatest. Betrayal thus takes place within the community's internal life relationships. Jesus speaks to this issue and teaches the early Christians that like him they must be people of service. Therein lies true greatness. Service is the basis and the attitude required for exercising the dominion which Jesus had received from the Father and transmitted to the church (22:29) in response to its loyalty (22:28).

Betrayal can also take place in relation to the community's threats and attacks from without. When Judas consummates his betrayal plans at the Mount of Olives, one of the disciples attacks with a sword and strikes the high priest's servant. However, Jesus reaches out to the man with a healing touch (22:51) and shows how his disciples must avoid the attitudes and methods of the betrayer, his co-conspirators and their accomplices (22:52-53).

In the second phase, we inquire why a classic Christian story is addressed to Christians today. To answer, we must look into our own betrayals, which may involve internal relationships as well as unchristian responses to an inhospitable world. Guided by Luke 22: 21-30, we examine ourselves as leaders and ministers in the church. Are we exercising authority like earthly rulers? Do we expect to be called people's benefactors? It cannot be that way with us (22:25-26a). Inspired by Luke 22:47-53, we confront our tendency to violence. Are we loyal to Christ in his selfless commitment to life? We must not attack our enemies with the "swords and clubs" of modern civilization (22:51-53).

A New Testament story may not spell out what we must do in our particular circumstances, but it does provide the norms for evaluating our attitudes and behavior and for seeking out the proper Christian response.

Where-When-Who-What-How-Why? With this final complex question, we examine how the story's formal elements, that is, the way it is told, and its material elements, namely, the spatial and temporal setting, the personages and their interaction, are related to the story's intentionality or purpose. With it, our synthesis is complete.

For example, Luke 4:16-30 is set in the Nazareth synagogue, the place where Jesus had been reared (Where), on a sabbath (When). The participants include Jesus and the members of the synagogue (Who). Jesus himself is at the center of the action, but the problem is that of the members of the synagogue in general. They expect Jesus' mission will be exercised on their behalf, but he affirms that, as in the biblical past, his mission will reach beyond them to the greater Gentile world (What). The synagogue responds with anger and violently tries to destroy Jesus. Their effort, however, is ineffective, and Jesus proceeds through their midst and walks away (What). In telling the story, the narrator structures its elements and movement after the pattern of Jesus' entire story, in which Jesus' mission leads to the passion, resurrection and ascension (How). The story is told to show the Lukan readers how the pattern of Jesus' life and the response he received illumines their own efforts and provides the grounds of hope even as many try to destroy them (Why).

In our own world, the story also provides a pattern for Christian existence and inspires fidelity (Why) to the church's universal mission, which will overcome all obstacles (What) as we continue the mission of Jesus in history (Who) and break away from the smallness and the exclusive tendencies which may be bound up with the human and religious institutions (Where) associated with our origins (When). Such will be the story's impact if we tell it or read it with the depth of perception which inspired its development (How).

Luke 10:38-42—The Application: After exploring the process of interpretation and the ramifications of the questions which we direct to New Testament stories, I shall now provide an example by applying the entire process to one particular story.

The story, which appears in Lk 10:38-42, is well-known. In the text of the New American Bible, it reads as follows.

> [38]On their journey Jesus entered a village where a woman named Martha welcomed him to her home. [39] She had a sister named Mary, who seated herself at the Lord's feet and listened to his words. [40] Martha, who was busy with all the details of hospitality, came to him and said, "Lord, are you not concerned that my sister has left me to do the household tasks all alone? Tell her to help me."

[41]The Lord in reply said to her, "Martha, Martha, you are anxious and upset about many things;[42] one thing only is required. Mary has chosen the better portion and shall not be deprived of it."

Where? The physical and geographical context of the story is complex, but all of its elements are interrelated.

Perhaps the reader has observed, first of all, that the event occurs in a village. That village, however, is along a journey, and within the village, we are in a house or home. Since serving and hospitality are indicated, we may go one step further and note that within the home we are in the dining area. The event is thus situated at table, in a home, in a village and along a journey.

The village is not specified as any particular village but is simply presented as a village. Its undefined nature gives it a certain universality, and as such the village could be any village. The home, however, is said to be that of Martha. It is thus a particular home, one which is distinguishable from the other homes in a village.

Readers should avoid reading Bethany into the text. This village may be associated with Martha in John 11:1-44, but Luke has avoided the name. Actually, Jesus is still in Galilee at this point on the journey, while Bethany is over the Mount of Olives in the immediate environs of Jerusalem.

The journey is a specific one and referred to as "their journey," an indication that Luke's readers are expected to know which journey is being referred to. The basis for this expectation is Luke 9:51, where Jesus' journey begins. In that verse, the journey is defined as a journey to Jerusalem, the place of the ascension. Others are with Jesus on this journey (9:57).

When? No date is given for the event. The time of day, however, can be inferred from the meal context. The Jews and early Christians used to gather for a meal at sundown, which marked the beginning of a new day (see Lk 24:29; Acts 20:7). For the rest, the meal could be on any day, and such potential universality should be noted.

Where-When? Since the journey to Jerusalem is viewed in terms of the ascension and consequently as a journey to God, our story is about a Christian meal on the journey to God in one of the villages where life unfolds and in a home where service and hospitality are expressed especially in table fellowship.

Who? The personages in the story include Jesus, those who journey with him, Martha and Mary. After the initial mention of those who accompanied Jesus, the followers do not figure in the story directly. Mention of them, however, indicates that the story concerns their journey with Jesus.

Martha, and not Mary, is the principal personage, and this is shown in the fact that the story takes place in her home and that Mary is introduced as her sister and not vice versa. Further, Martha alone joins in the dialogue, and she is the one whom Jesus addresses. Mary is simply a point of reference, albeit important, to whom both Martha and Jesus refer while she sits at Jesus' feet.

Where-When-Who? It is significant that the person engaged in service is Martha, a woman, and that the meal is in her home. She is thus the hostess for a meal with Jesus along the journey of Christian life. While at table, Mary is seated at Jesus' feet. She is in the traditional position of a disciple in the presence of a teacher. Martha, on the other hand, is busily going about, seeing to all the details of hospitality. The two women are thus carefully distinguished and positioned with regard to Jesus and one another.

What? From Martha's point of view, the problem is threefold. She has all the household tasks to do, her sister has left her alone to do them, and Jesus appears to be unconcerned about the situation. Her solution corresponds to this perception of her problem: Jesus should show concern by telling her sister to help her in doing all the household tasks.

Jesus, however, does not accept Martha's solution. In fact, he does not accept her assessment of the problem, which is not that she has too much to do but that she is anxious and upset about many things. So responding, Jesus is concerned, but about her real problem. Martha is avoiding the one thing which is required, and that thing is demonstrated in what Mary is doing, namely attending to the guest and listening to his words. Unlike Martha, Mary is communicating with Jesus within the teacher-disciple relationship.

Jesus does not tell Mary to cease doing what she is doing. Whether her behavior is altogether adequate is not the issue. In this story, what is important is that she demonstrates the one thing which is necessary and which is missing in Martha's attitude and behavior. Nor does Jesus tell Martha to desist from her activities. In performing these, however, she must avoid being anxious and upset, a condition which vitiates her activity and destroys its Christian focus.

Where-When-Who-What? Martha illustrates a problem concerning table fellowship which must be resolved among those who join Jesus in the Christian journey to God while engaged in the villages of life. If the journey is to remain on target, Martha, a leader in the Christian community, must attend to her problem. Since her home is not an ordinary home, but a place of Christian assembly, her responsibility is all the greater.

How? The narrator situates the event geographically and physically, introduces the personages and positions them with regard to one another. He also alerts us to the fact that this simple event in the life of the historical Jesus is about the journey of Jesus and those who accompany him. The introduction (10:38-40a) is extremely important and includes a smooth transition (10:40a) into the body, which consists of a dialogue between Martha and Jesus (10:40b-42), both of whom speak but once. The story concludes with Jesus' response, which is part of the body (10:41-42). No further conclusion is provided.

Jesus (see 10:37) is never referred to by his personal name. Twice, however, the narrator speaks of him as Lord (10:39, 41) and it is with this title that Martha addresses him (10:40). While the story ostensibly presents an event in the life of the historical Jesus, it is consequently about the life of the Christian community which, after the resurrection, relates to Jesus as Lord.

Where-When-Who-What-How? As the title Lord indicates, the author is not interested so much in those who accompanied Jesus in history as in those who pursue the Christian journey after his resurrection. Consequently, the story deals with a problem which arises in connection with the table of the Lord. The Christians have become anxious and upset as they see to the details of hospitality and have lost touch with the one thing which gives value to what they are doing, namely attentiveness to the Lord and his word. In this activity, they have forgotten that they are disciples and that they must attend personally to those through whom the Lord is present to them.

Why? Luke does not tell stories for their own sake. In view of the pastoral intention which guided both his selection of traditional stories and the way he presents them, we must assume that Martha's story was relevant for the Lukan churches of the 80s. Her problem mirrors one of their problems, and Jesus' response indicates the solution which should help them to refocus their values according to a genuinely Christian hierarchy. As is so often the case in Luke-Acts, the problem is one which affects the church's leadership and it surfaces in the Christian assembly for the breaking of the bread.

In our own times, the story is also told for its pastoral value. Are we like Martha, busy and anxious about the many details which surround our celebration of Eucharist? Are we avoiding the one thing which is necessary and which gives meaning to every other facet of the liturgy? Are we sensitive to the Lord's presence and to his word, both of which are sacramentally with us in the assembly, its members, our Liturgy of the Word and our eucharistic liturgy? Have these values been lost in our celebration? If so, is it more than a production, an external show uninspired by the Lord's presence and his word? Mary reminds us that in our initiatives we ever remain disciples at the feet of the master. When the apostle ceases to be a disciple, the entire apostolic task is emptied of Christian value.

Where-When-Who-What-How-Why? The one thing which is necessary, namely, attending to the Lord and his word, must penetrate our activities (Why, What) as we host the Christian community (Who) in the Eucharist (Where, When). As we read the story with sensitivity to its elements, values and movement (How), we realign ourselves on the Christian journey to God (Where).

The above method for analyzing a story is applicable to every story in the New Testament. It applies equally to the stories in the Old Testament. At times, one or another of the questions may be irrelevant. When this is the case, the fact should be noted and one should move on to the next question.

At all times, it is essential to maintain an open mind. Our observations are necessarily limited by our experience and present concerns. Later, on rereading the story, we may discover far more than we did during the previous reading. With this caution, the stories will always yield rich fruit and they will continue to mirror our Christian growth and development as we engage in the catechetical process.

Bibliographical Note

The literature on catechesis, and more specifically on catechesis in and through the scriptures, is understandably voluminous. For several decades, catechetical

106

renewal has walked hand in hand with the rediscovery of the scriptures in church life. Further, since the New Testament Gospels present Jesus as the model teacher or catechist, it stands to reason that Jesus' teaching ministry lies at the heart of much of our contemporary catechetical literature.

This bibliographical note focuses first on some of the major catechetical works of Christian antiquity. Second, it will review a number of scholarly approaches to Jesus' parable teaching and other questions of interest to the biblically inspired catechist. Third and finally, it will present some of the recent scholarly reflections on the art of Christian storytelling.

Few people in Christian history have combined extraordinary theological ability with pastoral sensitivity and astuteness in the measure evidenced by St. Augustine. Augustine's concerns were those of his time. The depth of his penetration, however, was such that his writings dominated the theological world until Thomas Aquinas in the 13th century. His influence persists. In our own day, this North African Christian and bishop is still classed among the very greatest of theological thinkers, and he remains a key participant in every discussion.

For catechists, Augustine's major work is his *On Christian Doctrine*, a study in four books which was intended as an introduction to the interpretation and explanation of the scriptures in a catechetical setting. The first three books stem from Augustine's earlier ministry. As Augustine states, these deal with the discovery of those things which must be understood. The fourth book, along with a few additions to the first three, was written toward the end of Augustine's life. It deals with the way of teaching the things which have already been grasped. Augustine's purpose in this additional book was to provide a primer of Christian eloquence. The Christian catechist and preacher had to model his manner of presenting the faith on the scriptures themselves, and not on the rules and the rhetoric taught in secular schools.

Augustine's distinction between the methods of discovering the meaning of scripture and of presenting it in Christian teaching prompted my own distinction between interpretation for understanding and interpretation for communication and expression. His turning to the scriptures for guidance in Christian eloquence led to my considerations of the witness of the New Testament before taking up the use of the New Testament in present-day ministry. His work can be found translated and introduced by D. W. Robertson, Jr. (New York: The Liberal Arts Press, 1958). The fourth book extends from page 117 to page 169.

No serious consideration of catechesis in Christian tradition can ignore the monumental contribution of St. Cyril of Jerusalem. As I noted while treating of evangelization, the first 18 of his catechetical lectures were destined for catechumens. The last five, however, which deal with baptism (19 and 20), confirmation (21), the Eucharist (22) and the liturgy of the faithful (23), were addressed to the newly baptized. These five, which are called the mystagogical catecheses, develop life's meaning for those who have entered the Christian mystery. They are presented in the form of commentaries and reflections on I Peter 5:8-14, Romans 6:3-14, 1 John 2:20-28, 1 Corinthians 11:23 and 1 Peter 2:1.

The author thus pursues the approach used in the earlier catecheses where scriptural texts provided a reference point for presenting the faith issues of his time.

In this process, the sacramental life of the Jerusalem church draws out the significance of the New Testament letters and the letters themselves cast their light on the sacraments. The five mystagogical catecheses can be found in *St. Cyril of Jerusalem's Lectures on the Christian Sacraments,* edited by F. L. Cross (London: S.P.C.K., 1951).

Parables constituted one of Jesus' most effective teaching methods. Their incorporation, reinterpretation and allegorization in the Gospel narratives guided and nourished the allegorization efforts of large segments of the church during patristic times, especially in North Africa and at Alexandria, where these efforts were extended from the stories told by Jesus to those which were about him. This interest in Jesus' parables and their influence persists in modern times.

One of the great contemporary works on the parables is Joachim Jeremias' *The Parables of Jesus* published by Charles Scribner's Sons (New York: 1972) in a second revised edition which is based on the eighth German edition (1970). As in the major part of his work on the New Testament, Jeremias' study of the parables is an effort to recover the historical setting in which Jesus spoke the parables. Only in this way can we discern Jesus' intention and the effect which the parables must have had on his hearers. After presenting the problem, the book includes two parts. In the first, the author shows how we can make our way back from the parables' New Testament literary context to the historical context of Jesus. In the second, he groups Jesus' parables into 10 categories and studies their message.

In *The Parables of the Kingdom* (London: Fontana, 1961), C. H. Dodd also sought the original context of the parables in the life of Jesus. Limiting himself to the parables which deal with the kingdom of God, Dodd reacts against the allegorical method. In his view Jesus' parables presented a single point of comparison. The details of the story, on the other hand, had no independent significance (p. 18). At the same time, he saw that the parables were "the natural expression of a mind that sees truth in concrete pictures rather than conceives it in abstractions" (p. 16). Sensing the tension between the two positions, more recent scholarship has abandoned the first, namely that parables have a single point of comparison, but vastly developed the fact that parables communicate in concrete pictures. Like Jeremias' book, that of Dodd is considered a modern classic.

John Dominic Crossan aligns himself with the quest of Jeremias and Dodd. His book, *In Parables* (New York: Harper & Row, 1973), is a study of the challenge of the historical Jesus. Sensitive to the nature of creative expression and its formal structuring, his focus is on how the parables spring from Jesus' experience as works of his creative imagination. Structured into an order which gives them credibility, they are expressed in poetic metaphor which bears on normal life situations.

Dan Otto Via, Jr., moved away from the efforts of scholars like Jeremias, Dodd and Crossan to situate parables in Jesus' historical setting. His contribution in *The Parables* (Philadelphia: Fortress, 1967) was rather to explore the parables as artistic or literary works through dialogue with aesthetic and literary-critical thought outside of biblical scholarship. With this approach, he shows how the parables transcended their original setting to become permanently significant. As such, they are stories whose many elements are related to one another in a manner which reflects a recognizable pattern of existence outside the story. Via's approach enables us to see how the parables are effective literary statements in any period of history including our own.

Parables had little place in St. Paul's teaching or catechesis. His interest was rather in the new law of faith, love and hope which corresponded to the life of Christians infused with the Spirit of the risen Lord. In a recent book, *Paul's Vision for the Teaching Church* (Valley Forge: Judson Press, 1977), David L. Bartlett examines Paul's view of the nature of the church which teaches, how it teaches and what it teaches. His book is an excellent contribution to our understanding of the church's ministry of catechesis. Emphasis on parables should not displace the approaches to teaching which Paul developed and which are part of the New Testament. Jesus himself did not teach in parables alone.

The study of Jesus' parables is closely associated with the more general approaches to storytelling in catechesis and theology. Amos N. Wilder, in *Early Christian Rhetoric: The Language of the Gospel* (Cambridge: Harvard University Press, 1971) devoted two chapters to the story and the parable in the New Testament. His emphasis on how both of these remain extremely close to spoken language enables us to move easily from the biblical text to the catechetical situation and to any other ministerial context where the living spoken word is the primary vehicle of communication. His work, originally published in 1964, has had a great influence on later authors such as Sallie TeSelle, who explored the theological implications of metaphor in *Speaking in Parables* (Philadelphia: Fortress, 1975). Chapter 6, "The Story: Coming to Belief," helps us to see how and why parabolic stories, which express the narrative structure of human experience, are so helpful in catechesis. Interest in this question leads us to the work of John Shea, *Stories of God* (Chicago: The Thomas More Press, 1978), a reflective and probing book which breathes with the spirit of one who has seriously committed himself to the biblical story in our time.

All three of the above works discuss the nature of the story and its place in ministry and theology. My own chapter supplements their efforts by showing how to proceed in the analysis of a New Testament story in catechesis.

Two recent commentaries on the New Testament will also assist the work of the catechist. The first is a Doubleday Image Book Original edited by Robert Karris. Its ten volumes with the text of the Jerusalem Bible, introductions, commentaries, study questions and suggested further readings may be described with the general title "Invitation to the New Testament." In this series, I have contributed the volume entitled *Invitation to the New Testament Epistles II,* which includes 1 and 2 Thessalonians, 1 and 2 Corinthians, Philippians and Philemon (Garden City: Doubleday, 1980).

The second commentary is the *New Testament Message* edited by Wilfrid Harrington and Donald Senior (Wilmington: Michael Glazier). Its 22 volumes include the text of the *Revised Standard Version,* introductions, commentaries and an annotated bibliography. In this series, I have contributed *Luke* (1980). The entire commentary's effort is to illumine the text of the New Testament in terms of the author's communication with the community he addresses.

112

3
The New Testament in Homiletics

The Eucharist is a living historical expression of God's word. From its initial welcoming to its final commissioning, the Christian community meets in a divine and human word to praise God, to celebrate the wonders of his creation, to marvel in gratitude at life's mystery, and to renew its commitment to the kingdom of God.

As multifaceted as life itself, this word-event is a proclamation of the death of the Lord until he comes (1 Cor 11:26). Accepting to live as Jesus lived, the community's voice is that of the Lord, a pledge of selfless and loving service to the entire human community's fulfillment in God's rule.

The Eucharist's highest interpretive and communicative moment comes in the community's personal acceptance of the Lord's word that this event is his body offered for all and his blood to be poured out for the forgiveness of sins. It is a moment in the history of the Christian covenant, a new set of divine and human relationships which transcends every societal, racial and class distinction.

In the Eucharist, the community thus joins in the Christian process of salvation. For the present, this means joining in Jesus' mission to bring good news to the poor, to proclaim liberty to captives, to open the eyes of the blind and to free the enslaved. At its historical term, when the Lord is fully come, the covenant seed will have matured into the perfect manifestation of the kingdom.

To join Jesus in his commitment, the community must have heard the Gospel and it must have learned what it means and implies. It must have been formed and reformed in God's word. Before it can commit itself to give its body and blood, the sacramental presence of the Lord's own body and blood, it must have heard his word in the uniqueness of its present moment of history. In the first part of the Eucharist, the community thus shares in the reading of the scriptures, and a member articulates the meaning and challenge of the biblical word in a manner which leads to a communal profession of faith and prayer. Such is the Liturgy of the Word, with its readings, meditative song, song of praise (Alleluia), homily, creed and prayer of the faithful.

This chapter concerns the homily and its interpretation of the scriptures. It presupposes that the community has been fundamentally evangelized and that its members stand at some point along the process of ongoing evangelization. It also presumes a basic catechesis in which the community has begun to understand its life as illumined by the scriptures.

Inspired by the Gospel's vision and informed by faith understanding, the homily has many elements in common with evangelization and catechesis. However, it cannot be reduced to these. The homily is a unique communicative event which is contextually defined by the Eucharist in which it is spoken. As such, the homily articulates the church's general eucharistic commitment for the present moment and in relation to the personal and social challenges which make it unique. It does this in relation to biblical texts whose import extends

114

beyond those challenges but includes them. The homily takes the texts' universal relevance and addresses their meaning for the eucharistic now of life.

The homily thus has two essential points of reference, the Eucharist and the scriptures. With regard to the Eucharist, it is part of the liturgy's spoken articulation of symbolic actions which define and express the very being and mission of the church. With regard to the scriptures, it joins the readings to give new and concrete life to a word which would otherwise remain a written and lifeless record of the church's origins and past history.

Neither of these points of reference can be ignored. For both the homilist and the assembly within which he or she speaks, they constitute the immediate life context, a context in which all participants are joined as one. The symbolic action and the living word thus provide the grounds for the kind of communication and sharing which are needed for a true homily.

The church's recent official teaching on homiletics is included primarily in the Second Vatican Council's Constitution on the Sacred Liturgy, *Sacrosanctum Concilium* (# 35, 52) and in the many decrees, instructions, declarations and apostolic constitutions which have been issued since its publication on December 4, 1963. Many of those which appeared before 1975 are conveniently published in *Vatican II, the Conciliar and Post Conciliar Documents*, edited by Austin Flannery (Northport, New York: Costello, 1975).

None of these documents is devoted entirely to the homily. The church's practice in this respect corresponds to its clear teaching that the homily is an integral part of the liturgy. With the rest of the Liturgy of the Word, it joins the eucharistic liturgy to "form but one single act of worship" *(Sacrosanctum Concilium,* # 56). This statement, which requires that the homily be understood in light of the liturgical event as well as in relation to the text of scripture, is the governing principle of this entire chapter.

The Witness of the New Testament

The New Testament is not a collection of homilies. Nor does it discourse on the nature of the homily and the pastoral ministry called homiletics. It does, however, provide an important witness for the homiletic interpretation of scripture.

The New Testament witness is threefold.

First, we have Jesus' scriptural interpretation of life in the context of synagogue prayer and reflection and in the course of various meals. As illuminative background for the Eucharist, these contexts approximate the eucharistic setting of the modern homily.

Second, we have the New Testament's many letters which were expected to be read in the Christian assembly, by someone other than the writer, who was unable to be present. The communicative setting of these letters corresponds to our own in that we too read and apply what someone else has written.

Third, we have the Gospel accounts, in which the evangelists retell the Christian story in a manner which addresses a specific community, evokes the vision of its origins, responds to its difficulties, shapes its attitudes, focuses its challenges and moves it to appropriate action.

Jesus as Homilist   Few passages in the New Testament illustrate the homiletic event as clearly as Jesus' inaugural presentation in the Nazareth synagogue (Lk 4:16-30).

First of all, Jesus is among his own people, and when he stands up to read and interpret Isaiah he does so as a member of the synagogue assembly (4:16). The reader and homilist do not stand over against the community. Rather, they present the word from within the community and give voice to the word of all.

Second, the text focuses on a scriptural passage which is proclaimed (4:18-19). In context this is a genuine announcement and proclamation. If the passage had been a story, it would not have been proclaimed. Stories are told and not proclaimed. To do otherwise vitiates their nature and destroys genuine communication.

Third, the author frames Jesus' scriptural reading with a number of seemingly meaningless actions which are described in precise detail. Jesus stood up to do the reading, the book of the prophet Isaiah was handed to him, he unrolled the scroll and he found the passage (4:16b-17). After the reading, the sequence is reversed. Jesus rolled up the scroll, gave it back to the attendant and sat down (4:20a). These details indicate deliberateness, focus attention, arouse expectations and highlight the importance of the moment. When Jesus has sat down, all in the synagogue have their eyes fixed on him (4:20b). All are united in spirit for the communication which is to follow.

Fourth, Jesus addresses those assembled to say that the word which they have heard is, that very day, fulfilled in their midst (4:21). The homily does not inter-

117

pret the word in its ancient context but as it now applies to those gathered.

Fifth, the reading and its initial application evokes wonder in the community and raises the question of Jesus' identity (4:22). The homily opens the eyes and ears of all in wonderment, discloses the homilist's Christian selfhood and invites all to penetrate the human surface of one they know in order to see into the mystery of his or her Christian existence. In so doing, they also open themselves to the recognition of their own Christian nature.

Sixth, Jesus then challenges the community to reach beyond itself into the greater world, where the Gospel must be proclaimed for the healing, liberation and reconciliation of all (4:23-27). The community does not receive the Gospel for itself but to share with others. The homily is thus a call to action. Unless the community is prepared to move outward to others, the Gospel will leave it behind. So threatened, it may turn to violence and lead its Gospel spokesperson to the cross (4:28-30a) in a futile effort to destroy the one who articulates that community's Christian selfhood (4:30b).

The many meals which Jesus shared with a variety of people, and particularly the Last Supper which he took with his disciples, also include statements and discourses akin to the homily. Among all of these, however, the various meals with the risen Lord found at the end of the Gospels according to Luke and John are the most significant. Specifically, our attention focuses on the dialogue which occurred along the journey to Emmaus (Lk 24:13-35). As an interpretation of the scriptures which leads to the breaking of bread, the event corresponds perfectly to the eucharistic context in which the homily has been shared throughout church history.

First, Jesus joins the disciples in their immediate situation (24:13-16). Unable to make sense or find hope in all that has happened in the passion and death of Jesus, a tragic series of events which has now been compounded by the empty tomb, the discouraged disciples have abandoned the way of Jesus (24:17-24). The homilist must listen to the Christian mood of the community and reach out to it in its actual situation. It would be futile to address the community as though all were well when all is not. The homilist's function is not merely to speak a message but to communicate, and for this he or she must meet the community's human and Christian state of mind.

Second, Jesus speaks to the disciples and reinterprets their inadequate understanding of the scriptures (24:25-27). Their view of Christian realities had not integrated Jesus' passion and death. He consequently broadens the base of interpretation to take in all of the scriptures and shows how they apply to himself and indirectly to them as well. The homilist thus expands the horizon of self-understanding to take in the whole reality of the community's life and challenge.

Third, the new understanding leads the disciples to reach out to the stranger in a gesture of hospitality (24:28-29). In the breaking of the bread, they recognize that this man is no mere Joseph's son (see Lk 4:22) but Jesus the risen Lord (4:30-31). Renewed in their faith, love and hope, the disciples' appreciation of the word event bursts into consciousness and they return to share the Gospel with those whom they had left behind on the way of Jesus (24:32-35). The homilist's word must likewise open the assembly to fellowship and hospitality, that it too might then eagerly spread the Gospel among those who have not been quickened by its word.

Letters in the Assembly Studies of the letters of Paul usually focus on their form, style and language, theology, message, historical context and the relationship of all these to emergent Christianity in the Jewish and Gentile world of the mid-first century. Rarely do such studies examine the specific context in which these letters were communicated and how this context influenced all the other aspects of the letters. In these pages, I shall reflect on their relationship to the Christian assembly and how this relationship contributes to our understanding of homiletics in New Testament times.

First, we must situate the letters within Paul's more general communication of the Gospel. Paul clearly did not think of himself primarily as a letter writer. For him, the Gospel message had to be shared through a Christian's personal presence and the living spoken word. Each of his letters attests to this when he assures his readers that he will come to them as soon as possible. He thus viewed his letters as temporary substitutes for personal communication, which alone could be considered adequate.

Why then did Paul write letters? In general, we can say that Paul's letters were born of a creative tension between the immediate needs of the Christian communities and the impossibility of his being personally present to them. From Paul's preaching of the Gospel, communities had sprung and grown in the major cities of the Aegean basin. This preaching had created a lasting bond. Because of it, the communities had a claim on Paul's attention and a need for his continuing mission, and he himself had a need to communicate with them. However, the enormous demands of his expanding mission, sporadic persecutions, divisive local situations and physical limitations made it impossible to fulfill this mutual need in person. Limited and inadequate as it might be, letter writing provided an alternate way.

Paul's letter writing closely approximated the personal word and presence for which it substituted. Concretely, this meant that the letters were to be read aloud, usually by someone who knew Paul well, and in the Christian assembly where Paul himself would have addressed the community. The inadequacies of communication by letter were thus minimized.

Paul's letters were meant to be read aloud by someone who could speak for Paul, interpret his message and answer questions in his place. Paul's expectations in this regard are well illustrated in Colossians 4:7-9. Writing in his own name and in that of Timothy (Col 1:1), the apostle begins by introducing Tychicus, the bearer of the letter, as "our dear brother, our faithful minister and fellow slave in the Lord." Tychicus will give the Colossians all the news about Paul. Indeed that is why he is being sent, in order that the Colossians might be comforted. Onesimus, another dear and faithful brother and a Colossian (see Philemon), accompanies Tychicus. Together they will inform Paul's hearers concerning all that was happening.

Similar expectations are expressed in Ephesians 6:21-22. Even if Ephesians did not come from Paul's own hand, together with Colossians, it witnesses to Paul's ordinary practice in the authentic letters. Paul's letters were never intended to be complete and comprehensive statements. On the contrary, Paul fully expected the reader to interpret and apply them to the local situation. The fact that Paul expected his emissary and reader to supplement the letters affected their nature.

The nature of Paul's letters and his intention in writing them provides a model for understanding the relationship between our liturgical readings and the homily. As in early Pauline communication, the homily extends the readings in the immediate situation and responds to local needs and interests which Paul could not have foreseen. In Paul's day, the apostle's absence was geographical. In our own, it is historical. When we read a Pauline passage and uncover its meaning and implications in the homily, we assume the role of Tychicus and Onesimus as well as of Timothy and Titus before them, and we enable Paul to cross the distance of time which separates him from us. Through his representatives, Paul continues to address Christians with whom he cannot personally be present.

The fact that Paul's letters were meant to be read aloud affected their form. Direct in tone, the letters use the various forms and techniques which were characteristic of a spoken address rather than of a work of literature. In reading them, we always sense a writer who imagined himself present to those he was addressing and speaking to them. We consequently appreciate them best when we approach them from the point of view of rhetoric.

As quasi-rhetorical documents, Paul's letters are eminently well suited to the liturgical situation in which we read them. A good reader thinks of himself or herself as speaking Paul's word to the community, not as one who is reading a literary text.

The reading and interpretation of Paul's letters took place in the Christian assembly. As we see from Acts

20:7-12, that is the ordinary context in which Paul himself addressed the communities when he could be personally present. His emissaries followed the same practice when they read letters from him and spoke in his name.

This practice is well attested in Colossians 4:15-16, where Paul asks that his letter be conveyed with his best wishes to the community at Laodicea and to the assembly that meets at Nymphas' house. The letter is to be read in the Laodicean assembly as well as in that of Colossae, and the Colossians are to read the letter which he sent to Laodicea in their own assembly. The fact that the letters were addressed to churches, and not to the various individuals which made up the churches, indicates that Paul's request to the Colossians corresponds to a general practice. The best time to address a church was when it was assembled.

One of the main functions of the assembly was to celebrate the Lord's Supper, or as Luke calls it, the breaking of the bread. From the beginning then, the liturgy provided the main context for reading Paul's letters. This is reflected in their content. Knowing that his letters would be read in the assembly, Paul greeted his readers with liturgical greetings such as "Grace and peace be yours" (1 Thes 1:1) or "Grace and peace be yours from God the Father and the Lord Jesus Christ" (2 Thes 1:2). His concluding blessings were also drawn from the liturgy: "The grace of the Lord Jesus Christ, and the love of God, and the fellowship of the Holy Spirit be with you all" (2 Cor 13:13). He quoted liturgical hymns (Phil 2:6-11), referred to the community's liturgical text (1 Cor 11:23-25) and alluded to the liturgical kiss of peace (1 Cor 16:20; 2 Cor 13:12). There can be little doubt that his letters were strongly influenced by developments which he had frequently presented in the context of a homily.

In keeping with their original context, Paul's letters can best be read today by one who fully shares in the liturgy and grasps its meaning and place in Christian life. The letters were written for sharing in the assembly of those to whom they were addressed. The renewed liturgy of our own time provides the life context in which their spirit and message is most perfectly actualized.

The Gospels and the Christian Story   All four of the New Testament Gospels were written during the last three decades of the first century. As historical narratives they speak of events which had taken place in the first three decades of that same century. As literary narratives, they select events from Jesus' history and gather them together in a consistent story, whose various parts reflect their author's sensitivity to the entire Christ event, which included his death and resurrection. As pastoral narratives, they tell Jesus' story in such a way that it mirrors the life situation of the people and channels their growth as communities and persons committed to Jesus' way to God and mission in history.

In all three respects, that is as historical, literary and pastoral narratives, the Gospels reflect our homiletic challenge and provide a model for addressing the community which has gathered for the Eucharist.

Like a Gospel writer, the homilist helps the community to reflect on its beginnings in the events of Jesus' life, death and resurrection. If the readings are well done, they will have evoked the community's vision of its origins. The homilist draws attention to those origins and reminds the community of its history. Again, like the Gospel writer, the homilist coordinates the various elements of the event or events into a communicative whole which articulates or at least suggests their relationship to the rest of the story. Finally, the homilist presents the event in a way which shows its relevance to the community. By speaking of the Gospel story as the story of the Christian community, he enables it to measure its life against the Gospel's classic expression, calls attention to departures from the norm and inspires the community to attune itself to the Gospel. The liturgy's call to unity in a self-sacrifice, which portrays in reality the self-sacrifice of Christ, assures that particular events will be seen in light of the climactic passion and resurrection.

An example from Luke 5:1-11 shows how this entire pattern and process is found in the story of Simon Peter's call to discipleship.

The Lukan story recalls an event in Jesus' life mission, during which he taught growing crowds by the Lake of Gennesaret. It is in that context that Jesus called his first disciples, including Simon who would one day be called Peter, and they left all to follow him. Since those disciples were fishermen, either Jesus or the very early retelling of the event saw the disciples' life story as one which moved from fishing for fish to fishing for men.

Luke situated this event in Jesus' general story at the beginning of a long literary development on the origins of the church's mission in that of Jesus (5:1-9:50). Aware of the leading role which Simon would one day assume and of his future position in the church as Peter or the Rock, he tells the story, not as the call of the first disciples as Mark had done (1:16-20). Rather, he tells it as the call of Simon (5:1-11) with whom a number of others were associated as partners in the fishing of men as they had been in fishing for fish (5:10-11). To show the continuity in the disciple's life, he presents him both as Simon (5:3, 4, 10) and as Simon Peter (5:8). To show the change in his relationship to Jesus, Luke has Simon address Jesus at first as "Master" (5:5). However, after the event in which Jesus' true identity is disclosed, Simon Peter addresses him as Lord (5:8). Peter's profession of faith in Jesus, an event which Mark disassociated from Peter's call (see Mk 8:27-30) is thus integrated in the very moment of his call.

As a pastoral message to the Lukan communities, the story shows how Simon had known Jesus prior to becoming his disciple. In those days, he had even helped Jesus to fulfill his mission, but not as one who personally assumed it (5:1-3). Such was the situation of the many who had come to know the Christians but had not yet entered the community. As a condition for coming to Christian faith, Peter had to follow Jesus' instructions in a situation which appeared humanly hopeless (5:4-5). On seeing the results, the extraordinary catch which came from obeying Jesus in defiance of fishing experience (5:6-7), Simon Peter recognized the enormous distance which separated him from Jesus and acknowledged his sinfulness (5:8-9). Jesus responds by calming his fears and announcing his mission (5:10), whose scope had been revealed in the overwhelming quantity of fish he and his partners had just caught (5:6-7). With that, they had the courage to leave all and follow Jesus the Lord (5:11). Such was the story and challenge of Luke's readers.

By retelling a story concerning the beginnings of the church and developing it literarily in light of the story's complete unfolding, Luke mirrored the story of the churches for which he wrote. In so doing, he provided security, inspired courage and calmed fears which had first been felt by no less than Peter.

The evangelists' retelling of the story in short episodes, which are integrated in the entire Gospel but which can also be considered individually, reflects the history of these stories in Christian tradition but it may also have been inspired by the liturgical context of the assembly in which the Christian stories were retold, reflected upon and applied to new situations. If this is so, the liturgical usage of these stories and their homiletic development corresponds to the Gospel writers' awareness and intention.

There can be no doubt that the Gospels frequently had the liturgy in mind and that it influenced these accounts. For Jesus, meals constituted privileged events for communication with his disciples and others. Meals would also play a like function in the life of the communities after his death and resurrection. Both historical factors help us to account for the Gospels' emphasis on meals in the story of Jesus. Their influence on the accounts is revealed, for example, in the stories of marvelous sharing, the multiplication of loaves, in which the fish which originally constituted a central element (Mk 6:34-44) were gradually moved to the periphery (Mk 8:1-10). This literary phenomenon parallels the liturgical development from the early practice of sharing a complete meal to the celebration of a symbolic meal with bread and wine. For such Christian communities, mention of fish in the multiplication account was less and less significant. Luke even resituated the story in an urban setting in which the participants were grouped at tables (Lk 9:10-17). His urban dwellers would have found it far more difficult to identify with the desert hillside of the original story.

The New Testament no doubt includes many other elements which witness to the nature and function of homiletics in the earliest church. Those we have selected, namely, the presentation of Jesus in homiletic or quasi-homiletic situations, the practice of reading and developing Paul's letters in the Christian assembly, and the very nature of narrative communication in the Gospels suffice to provide a basis for our considerations on preaching the New Testament in the liturgy.

Preaching the New Testament in the Liturgy

After the Gospel reading and before the community profession of faith and the prayer of the faithful, the liturgy calls for a homily. These formal elements in the Liturgy of the Word are organically related in a simple and natural Christian process. At least, that is the way things are meant to be. After hearing the scriptural word, the assembly should feel a definite need for the homily, and if the homily itself has met the assembly's felt need, the assembly should experience the further need to profess its faith and to pray. Liturgical preaching is thus an integral element in the Liturgy of the Word. Together with the other elements in the first major portion of the liturgical celebration, it leads to the Lord's Supper or Eucharist proper.

The way we understand the liturgy and the function which the homily plays within it determines the homily's approach to the New Testament's Gospel and accounts for the distinction between homiletic interpretation and the general modes of interpretation which are appropriate for evangelization, catechesis and prayer outside the liturgical context.

In modern times, the church has embarked on a major renewal of the eucharistic liturgy. This effort stands at the heart of an even broader program of church renewal. The facets of this renewal are many, and they affect every single aspect of the liturgy. From the point of view of the homily, however, the most significant shift concerns the relationship between the priest celebrant and the Christian assembly.

For centuries, we perceived the Eucharist as the priest's action. At bottom, it was Christ's action, of course, but Christ acted in and through the person of the priest. The people were seen to attend the Mass, with the result that they remained liturgically passive. In the decades which preceded the Second Vatican Council, however, we began to perceive the Eucharist as the action of the entire Christian assembly. This new appreciation was confirmed by the Council, so that Christ is now seen to act in and through the assembly. The priest celebrant is viewed as one who presides at the Lord's Supper, who leads the assembly in worship and articulates an event which engages all the participants.

This shift in appreciation and emphasis has enormous repercussions on the way the liturgy is celebrated. With regard to the homily, it repositions the homilist as one who illumines and focuses the word of God which has already been shared with the community. No longer should the homilist stand over against the assembly. Speaking from within it, he becomes the voice of the entire community in a communal effort to interpret the biblical word.

The shift in appreciation and practice is reflected in shifts in language. Whereas we used to speak of the Mass, we now tend to speak of the liturgy, the Lord's Supper or the Eucharist. Whereas we used to speak of the sermon, we now speak of the homily, and the word "sermon" has all but fallen into disuse, at least in areas where the liturgical renewal took hold and is well advanced.

The reality, of course, is the same, but new awareness calls for new language. Our change in language springs from the realization that the eucharistic reality and the relationships among the participants are experienced differently.

The terms "sermon" and "homily" both refer to a human discourse which is uttered in a religious context and more particularly as part of a worship service. Our sermons, however, tended to be more theological or dogmatic than our homilies, which are always scriptural, both in their point of departure and in their development. A sermon, for example, could be on the dogmas of the Immaculate Conception and Assumption, and its development might have touched on the scriptures only tangentially. The homily, on the other hand, remains close to the day's scripture texts, and the dogmatic considerations associated with a feast such as the Immaculate Conception become tangential.

The term "sermon" also connotes a formal presentation and is associated with the church's long rhetorical tradition. The term "homily," on the other hand, indicates a more informal and spontaneous sharing. These characteristics have nothing to do with poor preparation or lack of quality in the presentation. On the contrary, a successful homily requires far more preparation than a sermon. The difference lies in the homilist's close attention to the community's visual and bodily response, which contributes to the homily's development. For this to be possible, the homilist must be sensitive to the listeners and the homily's preparation must be open-ended, allowing the homilist to respond to the congregation's simultaneous and continuous feedback. This means that whereas a sermon's text may have been fixed definitively before its delivery, the homily's text is not completely finalized until its last word has been spoken.

The homily can thus be described as a conversation. Primitively, both the homily and the sermon were viewed as conversations in their respective Greek and Latin contexts. In the course of history, however, the sermon lost this quality, at least in general. Today's shift to the term "homily" restores this ancient perception and rejoins an important element in Christian tradition.

In these pages, I shall consider three distinct questions related to the use of the New Testament in a homily. If the homily is a kind of conversation, how does this affect New Testament interpretation? How should the homily deal with the two or three readings specified by the liturgy? How does a particular Sunday's homily relate to those which are shared on the other Sundays in a liturgical season? The first of these questions concerns primarily the homily's relationship to its liturgical point of reference. In the second and third questions, the main concern is the homily's relationship to its scriptural point of reference.

The Homily as Conversation   A good conversation involves the entire person of those who participate in it, and it requires that they communicate simply and directly. It presupposes that the participants have a common ground, that they not be afraid to relate to one another, and that the topic be both subjective and objective. A good conversation deals with the participants' perceptions, views and attitudes concerning the subject of common interest. The same is true of a good homily.

The common ground which unites the homilist and the rest of the assembly consists in the Gospel in which they were evangelized and catechized. Fundamentally, it springs from their shared Christianity, from their having the same basic Gospel mission and vision. More immediately, it stems from the faith, love and hope which have drawn the participants into the assembly for the Lord's Supper. Most immediately, it is established by the liturgical readings and responses which comprise the first part of the Liturgy of the Word. For this to be so in fact as well as in principle, the readings must have been truly shared; that is, well read and actually heard. A high quality of liturgical reading is thus of paramount importance for a good homily.

From the point of view of the reader, the liturgical relationship among the participants requires that the readings have been internalized. The scriptural message must have become incarnate in the reader, whose person and life must be penetrated by the values and meaning inherent in what is read. The reader must be like Ezekiel, who had been asked to eat the scroll of God's word, so that the word of God would no longer be distinguishable from his own (Ez 2:8-3:3).

The readers must also be vitally interested in the participants. Before reading the text, the readers should ask themselves whether those who have gathered for the liturgy mean anything to them. In general, the answer to this question will be affirmative, but it does not suffice to ask the question in general. What of now and here, in this church, and these particular people: do we love them? Before telling Simon to feed his sheep and lambs, Jesus asked whether Simon loved him (Jn 21:15-17). Can we now hear the Lord's voice in our brothers and sisters? Peter, Gary, Claudette, Gene, do you love me? Asking this question of ourselves and answering it will prepare us to read as we should and will ensure a common ground for the homily.

From the point of view of the reading itself, it matters that we respect the nature of the text. If the reading is a story, it must be read as such. To do so well, a process of preparation such as I outlined and illustrated in the chapter on catechesis will prove helpful. Readers will then avoid the temptation of proclaiming the story. Instead they will think of themselves as telling it. Proclamation is closely associated with the Gospel in New Testament tradition, but this is due to the fact that the Gospel proclamation is the first stage in the development of a Christian community. It has little to do with the nature of Christian stories, which presuppose that the Gospel has been proclaimed.

The reading, of course, may consist of a proclamation or an analogous prophetic text. In this case, it should be proclaimed. A story like Luke 4:16-30 includes a proclamation (Lk 4:18-19). Its liturgical reading calls for a good storyteller (Lk 4:16-17, 20-30) who can also proclaim Jesus' prophetic message (Lk 4:18-19).

If the text develops an important issue, argues for a particular position or tries to inspire genuine values, as is so often the case in Paul's letters, the tone of the reading must vary accordingly. In these cases, the reader must identify with Paul and his purpose, recognize the key points in his development and present these with different emphases, so that the force and the nuances of Paul's statement are well communicated.

When the readers have internalized the passage which is to be read and when they are keenly interested in communicating this passage to a community whom they love, they are bound to experience a certain frustration at having to read the text. The book then becomes a barrier between the readers and the assembly. The resulting tension, which may first be felt in a situation where communication is vital, is extremely healthy and creative. If it is not dismissed and the desire to communicate is not abandoned, it will lead the reader to memorize the text. Freed from the book, the reader then speaks the message or tells the story with the directness which the situation requires.

In other fields and areas of life, people willingly memorize a message for a more effective communication. The same should not appear extraordinary for something as important as the liturgy, especially on special occasions.

The alternative to memorization would be to abandon the scriptural text and to present the biblical message in one's own words. The reading would thus become the homily. However, the community would be deprived of the classic formulations of the Christian story and message. The presence of these texts in the New Testament and their acceptance as such by the church reflects the universal judgment that the Gospel writers have presented a story in a good and truly Christian way. Each account of the empty tomb, for example, while different from the others, presents Jesus' resurrection in a manner which is relevant to all Christians, everywhere and for all time. Had we been among the eyewitnesses, our telling of the story might well have fallen short of their classic statements.

By retaining the wording of the scriptures in a good and tested translation, we align ourselves with a normative text and enable our congregation to ground itself in the tradition of the universal church. We thus preserve our communities from the spiritual under-nourishment which might stem from the reader's human and Christian limitations.

The kind of reading we have described establishes a common ground which binds all the participants, including the homilist, in a shared experience of the Gospel. For the homily to be conversational, however, it is also necessary that he and the assembly not be afraid to relate to one another. Such openness cannot be assumed, for the readings, if they were well presented, should have unveiled our common limitations, weaknesses and sinfulness. These are especially obvious when the homilist and the participants know one another in daily life.

To relate to the assembly, the homilist must be humble. He must be willing to recognize and accept his failings and limitations. So doing, he will not fear the congregation's negative judgment of him. If he truly loves the people he is addressing, this should not be so difficult.

The recognition of one's limitations is a matter of personal attitude. It does not require that these become the subject of the homily. This would merely indicate that the homilist is struggling with his Christian identity and is using the community to unburden himself. Such narcissism has nothing in common with humility. If the homilist views himself as a member of the assembled community, he finds no need to exalt himself above the others. A good and humble self-image is obvious to the entire community.

We now come to the topic or subject of the homily. It is here that its distinctive features as a form of New Testament interpretation emerge.

First, we should state that the homily is not about the text in itself, either as memorized or as it rests in the book of the New Testament. Nor is it about the homilist's analysis and understanding of the scripture text or about someone else's grasp and appreciation of it. A homily is not an exposition of the text, an exegetical exercise (understanding it in its New Testament context) or a hermeneutical interpretation (understanding it for its present-day context). These are extremely important, but all three are presupposed by the liturgy and its homily. They belong to the domain of biblical studies and theology.

Nor is the homily about the community's various understandings of the scriptural word. In this case, the homily's intended conversation would dissolve into a discussion or dispute concerning what the text can or does mean. Again, such discussion is important, but it too is presupposed by the homily. It belongs to the domain of catechesis.

The homily is about the word which has already been read and heard and which now lives in the faith of the assembled community. It is about the new incarnation of the scriptural word which has just been realized through the reading. The homily is thus not about the word which was to be read but about the word which has been heard. Its concerns are both objective and subjective. They deal with the objective text's subjective perception in the faith of the community at a particular moment in its development.

Homilists read the text in the eyes and on the features of the assembly. They deal with the word which is now inscribed on the hearts of the faithful. Their function is manifold. First, they must perceive the living word accurately and sensitively, and they must help the community to articulate that word. For this, the entire liturgical context with its symbols, physical disposition and eucharistic space provides a ready resource. They must also help the community overcome any resistance it might have to the word which it has received. In this, they act as prophets, the voice and conscience of the community, which help the community not only to hear the word but to accept it and appropriate it as its own. Finally, they assist the community in discerning what the word requires of it and how it must act upon it.

In this process, the community itself, the living church, becomes an essential element in the text's interpretation. In a sense, it represents a rewriting of the Gospel, providing it with all the concreteness which it possessed in the New Testament period. The ancient Galilean and Judean settings become the place of assembly. Sabbaths and feasts become Sundays and the great feasts of the liturgical year. The participants in the Gospel drama, with its disciples and apostles, rich and poor, men and women from all walks of life, become the community assembled to celebrate the Eucharist. With this attitude, the homilist develops the New Testament stories and the challenging words of Paul through their new incarnation in the Christian assembly.

The Homily and Several Readings   On Sundays and solemnities, the Liturgy of the Word includes three readings. Of these, the first is usually from the Old Testament, the second from one of Paul's letters, and the third from one of the Gospel narratives. Since this is the normal context for the homiletic experience of most Christians, it is here that my reflections will focus, rather than on the weekday liturgy which contains only two readings.

The three readings present the homilist with two major problems. First, the very fact that there are three seems unmanageable. One reading, such as the Gospel, is a difficult enough challenge. How can the homilist possibly cope with three or even two? The table of the word appears far too generously laden. How can the assembly possibly accept and share so much? In many if not most cases, marvelous portions are simply left untouched.

The second problem comes from the choice of the readings. Whereas the Old Testament and the Gospel readings are usually quite clearly related, the reading from Paul appears totally disconnected from the other two. During major seasons, such as Advent and Lent, and on special solemnities, such as Christmas and the Ascension, this is not so. However, on ordinary Sundays, it certainly is true. As with the Gospels, the church takes one of the epistles and presents its most important units sequentially on a series of consecutive Sundays. The liturgy's intention is to expose the community to the epistle itself, without regard for the theme found in the first and third readings.

Confronted with these problems, the homilist tends to follow one of several courses. The first may be to focus on one reading and ignore the others. Usually the reading selected is the Gospel, especially when it is drawn from one of the synoptics. Since many find John difficult and repetitious, when this Gospel is used on several consecutive Sundays the tendency is to concentrate on the first or second reading. A second course is to focus on the first and third readings, which are thematically related, and to ignore the second. In both of these cases, the question naturally arises as to the importance of the readings which are ignored. If they constitute no more than a liturgical incumbrance, why not avoid reading them altogether? Is not our current practice a subtle communication that they are irrelevant? Are we not doing an injustice to these works which we nevertheless present as important expressions of God's word?

A third course is to try to deal with all three readings. In this case, the homilist moves from one reading to the next. Since the second reading is not usually connected with the others, the tendency is to present two or three homilies, one following the other. Even if the homilist manages to show a relationship among all three readings, the effort leads to a long and frequently cumbersome development. He thus adds further fare to a table which already appears overladen, and the community, for all its good will, risks liturgical indigestion.

These problems, which stem from the structure of the liturgy and the richness of the readings, can be overcome and their pitfalls avoided. To do so, however, one must have a keen sense of the nature of the homily as we described it in the previous section. I doubt that they can be resolved when the homily is viewed as an exposition or discourse on the scripture texts in themselves. Prior to the liturgical renewal, when we gave and heard a sermon instead of a homily, we did not even try to deal with one whole reading. The preacher used to begin by quoting a single verse from one of the texts of the day and proceed to deliver his sermon on that verse. In this context, both the epistle and the Gospel, which then constituted the liturgical readings, appeared irrelevant.

First, it should be noted that the three readings are not meant to be taken on the same plane. The principal reading is that of the Gospel, which provides the immediate launching pad for the homily. It is consequently altogether appropriate that the homily deal primarily with the Gospel and the way it has been received by the assembly.

The second most important reading is the one which introduces all three, a reading from the Old Testament or the book of Acts. The function of this reading is to provide a general framework within which the Gospel is later situated. For example, an Old Testament reading might present the Israelite covenant at Sinai, a covenant which is specified in the Gospel as the covenant in Christ's blood. Or again it might describe a traditional context of hospitality which prepares the assembly to consider the way Jesus' words and deeds reveal the meaning and implications of this hospitality for Christians. The function of this first reading is primarily to create an atmosphere and to elicit a general reaction. At the more conceptual level, it also discloses a historical promise which is fulfilled in the Gospel. The danger is to dwell exclusively on this second level and to ignore the first.

The second reading comes third in importance. Even when it is thematically unrelated, it forms an important part of the Liturgy of the Word. Its function is to focus the first and third readings on a particular issue with which every community must deal. For the most part, this issue is one of ethics and Christian self-understanding. For example, if the first and third readings focus our attention on the presence of God and the presence of Christ in history, the second may deal with a condition or set of attitudes which are needed to perceive these. The theme of presence thus becomes related to issues such as faith, love, hope, openness to strangers, sensitivity to the poor, the implications of baptism, or the mission of the church. Part of the homily's preparation is to uncover this relationship.

It must also be noted that the homilist should view the readings in the order which corresponds to their respective functions. In the mind and attitude of the homilist, this order moves from the third reading to the first and then to the second. However, this is not necessarily the order in which he develops the homily. He could, for example, move from the presence of God, the Sinai covenant or Abraham's hospitality (first reading) to their specific embodiment and transformation in Jesus' mission, death and resurrection (third reading) and then consider an ethical concern which is related to them (second reading). What is important is that their natural order and function be clear in the homilist's mind and be respected.

The first reading is a preparatory text. Whether the homilist treats it first, second or third, it must be seen as a background statement and not as the climax of the liturgy's message, which is in the Gospel. If it is presented in first place, its general nature and tension toward further fulfillment must be apparent. If the Gospel is presented first, the assembly should be able to recognize that it was not without preparation (first reading) and ethical implications (second reading).

Examples from the theater or music may prove helpful. Before a play or opera begins, the curtain opens, and the lighting may focus exclusively on the chief participants, with all else clothed in darkness. After a few seconds, the background is illumined, and

141

the protagonists are visually situated in a general context. Still later, a spotlight may bring out the villain or some of the other problematic elements in the situation. The order of presentation would thus follow a homiletic pattern which begins with the Gospel, situates it against its Old Testament background and then calls attention to an ethical concern. An altogether different order could have been followed. In any case, there would be no mistaking how the elements, that is, the protagonists, the background and the problem or foil, are in fact related to one another.

Third, the homily should focus on one or another of the readings. While respecting the natural order in which the readings complement one another, it remains possible to provide a greater development for one of them. This is obvious in the case of the Gospel. However, it may be that, due to special needs and background of the community, one of the other readings should command the homilist's attention. The criterion in this case is that of pastoral need.

If the homilist is conscious of the intended relationship among the readings, his chosen focus will not ignore the other readings, but simply provide the angle from which they are viewed and developed. The readings already should have provided a good oral interpretation of the texts. When this is the case, the three readings join in a synthesis within the faith of the community. For example, it sees the new covenant established at Jesus' Last Supper (third reading) against the background of the Sinai covenant (first reading) and senses how behavior can be at odds with the attitudes which these call for (second reading).

By focusing on one of the readings, the homilist recognizes that he need not articulate every aspect of their synthesis. One reading, or even one element in it, could also provide a key to the internalization of all the others. In Christian life, growth in any one area leads to growth in every area. With regard to the implications for the community's renewal and mission, priorities must be established and an orderly program of action undertaken.

By retaining the other readings, even when they are not the focus of the homily, the community is left with a need for further reflection and exploration. At the liturgy's close, it will have dealt with some of the questions on its Christian agenda, but it will also realize that its agenda is unfinished and in fact open-ended. A well-focused homily will thus have contributed to the ongoing and lifelong process of the community's development.

The Homily and Liturgical Seasons   The very fact that the church has selected three readings, taken them from their distinct literary contexts in the scriptures, and brought them together into a new relationship within the Liturgy of the Word constitutes an interpretive judgment. It is in this new context that the readings energize and orient the life of the church community. In this respect, the church stands *vis-a-vis* the scriptures in the same way that Paul and the Gospel writers stood with regard to the traditions or writings which preceded them. What is true of each Sunday and solemnity is equally true of the Liturgy of the Word for entire liturgical seasons.

In Advent and Lent, as well as in the Christmas and Easter seasons which follow them, the church presents us with new syntheses of the whole biblical tradition. In doing this, it is guided by the Gospel texts which follow one another from Sunday to Sunday like individual pericopes in our New Testament Gospels. Like the story units in the Gospels, each Gospel reading can be approached on its own and examined in its uniqueness. These units, however, are not fully comprehensible unless we see them in their relationship to the whole Gospel and note what they contribute to it.

This insight from present-day literary analysis in New Testament studies helps us to appreciate what the church intends in a liturgical season. Each Sunday Gospel stands on its own and the homily may treat it as such. Much will be lost, however, including the dynamic development of the season, if we fail to consider a Sunday Gospel's relationship to the other Sunday Gospels in a particular season. Taken together, the season's Gospel readings constitute the church's own Advent, Lenten, Christmas or Easter Gospel, each of which is as distinctive as the Gospel narratives according to Matthew, Mark, Luke and John.

In establishing a season's sequence of Gospel readings, the church is guided by two principles or criteria. First there is the nature of the season. Accordingly, Advent approaches the New Testament Gospels from the point of view of the church's expectations and yearning for the coming of Christ. Christmas approaches them from the point of view of the fulfillment of these expectations and the church's consequent responsibilities. Lent and Easter are much like Advent and Christmas, both in their respective uniqueness and in their relationship. In Lent, however, the church looks to the coming of the risen Lord, an event which will be accomplished through Christ's passion and death. In keeping with the season, the readings focus on conversion and penitential preparation for the resurrection. In the Easter season, it celebrates the resurrection and examines its implications for Christian life.

The second criterion is the church's own position in the history of salvation. Jesus was born long ago and rose as Lord but a few years afterwards. For the church, this event constitutes the ancient history in which it came to being. Accordingly, when Advent looks forward to Christ's coming, the church's hope is fixed on his final coming and manifestation at history's consummation and complete fulfillment. When Lent looks forward to Christ's resurrection, it looks beyond the resurrection to Christ's departure from history and to the time when the church would be responsible for continuing his historical mission. The two preparatory seasons thus begin with a Gospel text concerning the return of the Lord and his intermediate absence from history, and they continue with readings aimed at preparing his return and at life during his absence.

The Christmas and Easter seasons present the new life which was engendered in the incarnation and the resurrection and how the church is enriched and challenged by that life as it celebrates Christ's final coming in eager anticipation. With these perspectives, the church avoids the nostalgic sentimentality which these seasons would otherwise arouse. When we celebrate a birthday, we do not actually celebrate the day of our birth but the life which has unfolded from it and our hopes for the future. So also with the church as it celebrates Christian beginnings.

With the sequence of Gospel texts as our guide, we can then examine how the first and second readings contribute to the seasonal Gospels. For this we need only recall the reflections and principles presented in the above treatment of the homily's relationship to the three readings. The first and second readings for the various Sundays do not constitute independent sequences in themselves. They were selected purely in relation to the Sunday's Gospel reading.

Two considerations for homiletic interpretation emerge from these observations on the seasonal readings. First, the assembly will be greatly enriched if the homilist introduces the entire season on its first Sunday, thus providing the assembly with a sense of the whole. Each Sunday clearly will be seen as one of its building blocks. The momentum which is thus generated will be maintained if at the end of the homily the homilist indicates how it is related to that of the following Sunday. Then on the second Sunday, he might do well to recall the previous Sunday in the introduction to his homily and end with a reference to the following Sunday. Through this process which is inspired by the church's structuring of the seasons, the homilist will meet the experience of people who are largely accustomed to serialized presentations on television. In this, the best point of reference is not the regular weekly program whose serialization is superficial and whose episodes go nowhere, but the weekly news analyses or journals, which usually begin by referring to the report given on the previous week, which indicate reactions to it, and which end by announcing some of the high points of the following week's program. Like the homily, such programs must also take into consideration events which occurred during the intervening week. Let it not be said that the children of this world are wiser than those of the kingdom!

Second, since it frequently happens that the homilist for the same liturgical celebration varies from

Sunday to Sunday the season should be planned as a whole by the liturgical planning team or committee. In this way, people will benefit from a variety of insights and approaches without suffering from discontinuity.

Preaching the New Testament in the liturgy is no easy task. As a church, however, we surely can rise to its challenge. These reflections have focused on the homily as a conversation with the assembly, on how to deal with the three readings constructively and realistically and on situating individual Sunday homilies in the more general seasonal patterns. If they are helpful, they will lead to further reflections, from which better and more useful approaches will be generated.

Bibliographical Note

The many books and articles on preaching in general and on homiletics or liturgical preaching which continue to appear in modern times witness to the sad state of preaching in the church as well as to the recognition that something can and must be done about the situation. It seems to me, however, that many of the publications fail to grasp the full import of the problem.

At its deeper levels, the problem springs from the homily's relationship to the liturgy and to the scripture texts. It is consequently twofold.

Much of the current writing is insensitive to the liturgical nature of preaching and to the homily's relationship to the total liturgical context. This insensitivity may stem from a writer's overspecialization in homiletics or scripture. However, it can also stem from the way the liturgy is viewed in a particular church. If the homily or sermon is considered to be the high point of the worship service, as in many Protestant churches, the problem is understandable. Indeed, it is not a problem for the Protestant who functions, as he or she must, in that tradition. However, it is a problem for the Catholic or for anyone who preaches in a church where the liturgy as such and the Lord's Supper play the dominant and central role.

A good effort to situate the homily liturgically can be found in Gilbert E. Doan, Jr.'s contribution to *Preaching the Story*, edited by Edmund A. Steimle, Morris J. Niedenthal and Charles L. Rice (Philadelphia: Fortress, 1980). His chapter is entitled "Preaching from a Liturgical Perspective" (pp. 95-106). Like the rest of this book, which is excellent, Doan approaches liturgical preaching from the point of view of storytelling. The liturgy itself is seen to have a narrative structure, and the homilist's role is to articulate it. However, the liturgical story is viewed almost exclusively in terms of the divine-human relationship, of what we might call its vertical dimension. Its horizontal dimension, through which the liturgy gathers up the Christian community's life and relationships and propels the community outward into the Christian mission, is almost absent. As a result, the liturgical story appears uprooted from its human context and totally absorbed into the divine.

From a contemporary Catholic point of view, John Burke's chapter, "The Liturgical Homily," in his book *Gospel Power, Toward the Revitalization of Preaching* (New York: Alba House, 1978), pp. 77-87, appears better balanced. It too is very sensitive to the liturgical context. As Burke indicates, "The homily is a short sermon integrally related to a liturgical act which inspires the worshipper to participate in the liturgy more fully in faith" (p. 78). The purpose of this is that "The effects of the sacrament extend beyond the immediate sacramental celebration into all phases of their daily life and the life of the entire church" (p. 79). One of his major points, that a good homily is neither an impromptu speech nor a manuscript speech, but an extemporaneous one which is carefully prepared but open-ended (pp. 81-84), coincides with the position I have taken.

The second problematic area is the homily's relationship to the scripture texts. At this point, much of the literature is again fairly disappointing. Authors tend to focus too heavily on exegesis or hermeneutics, as though a grasp of these is all that is required from the point of view of interpretation.

Some recent works recognize the limitations of exegetical and hermeneutical forms of interpretation for homiletics. In order to correct the imbalance, they emphasize the need for using images and religious language in the homily, as the New Testament itself does. A book by James M. Reese, *Preaching God's Burning Word* (Collegeville: The Liturgical Press, 1975), is a fine theological and inspirational contribution to this general effort. George R. Fitzgerald's book, *A Practical Guide to Preaching* (New York: Paulist Press, 1980), is more practical, as the title indicates, than theological. Although he recognizes the limits of exegesis for homiletics, he has few suggestions to supplement these in the order of interpretation.

Along with the theoretical and practical works on homiletics, the post-Vatican II era has also seen a proliferation of homiletic services, many of which are excellent. By providing the prospective homilist with shortcuts and sometimes with prepackaged homilies, however, they may unwittingly contribute to another kind of problem. Reliance on the materials provided might alleviate the homilist's heavy schedule, but it does not allow for internalizing the message or for attunement to the particular needs and attitudes of the community.

It is with this problem in mind that I published *The Year of Luke* during the past year (*Celebration Books*, Kansas City: National Catholic Reporter, 1979). Much of this book was first published as "Biblical Backgrounds" in *Celebration*. Besides an introduction to Luke's Gospel, to each major season, and to each Sunday and solemnity, I provided a brief commentary on the three readings and gave a number of homily suggestions. The book is especially helpful when it forms the basis for a discussion in a liturgical planning group and is used along with the scripture texts to prepare the homily. *The Year of Matthew* and *The Year of Mark* will both soon be made available by the same publisher.

4
The New Testament in Prayer

Prayer is a human being's spontaneous response to God. Born of the experience of God, it wells up in the human spirit as soon as one becomes aware of the divine presence and of his or her human creatureliness. For Christians, it speaks to God's presence in Christ, the human mediation of God's love for sinners. Prayer is the response of human beings and Christians whose true self has been unveiled by the divine presence and who have accepted this divine disclosure.

Prayer is the most delicate of all Christian activities, the one which allows no room for dishonesty. Whenever we are unable to confront ourselves as we truly are, the fire of prayer is extinguished. As our mind wanders, we eventually discover that the air which surrounds us has become cold and that strange, distracting and disquieting currents have enveloped us. In our escapism, we have lost touch with the Gospel word which sparked life's flame. God is gone, and prayer is no more.

Prayer, this spontaneous and delicate activity, is one of the primary functions of Christian life, an activity in which the church and its members express their identity before God and listen to his creative and saving word. As an expressive function, it recognizes that as Christians we are radically needy and it acknowledges willingness to be God's agents in fulfilling our own needs and the needs of all. As a listening function, it

151

perceives our Christian identity as unfolding and opens itself to the progressive discovery of our true needs.

As an expressive and listening function, prayer does not involve Christians in a communicating process with other human beings. Unlike evangelization, catechesis and homiletics, it is consequently not a communicative function of church life, at least not in the same sense as these others.

From another point of view, however, it is a form of communication in which Christians address God out of faith, in love of neighbor and with hope, and in which God reveals himself. In this communication, faith and divine revelation are correlatives. Faith and divine revelation, however, are not matters of spirit alone. God reveals himself in the created universe of inanimate wonders, living beings and Christian commitments. Faith meets him in the heavens, in the tiny bud, in a searching and yearning people and in the eyes of those who have found new life in Christ.

Analytically, the pattern of prayer is that of dialogue. God speaks to his people and they speak to him. In reality, however, the two terms of the dialogue coincide in one and the same word, which is both human and divine. In the very act of speaking to God, we hear him speak to us.

As a human and divine word, the New Testament provides classical and tested language for our spontaneous response to God. Its language formulates the present stage of our emergence as Christians, brings our limited self-realization to awareness, and draws us forward toward the fullness of life in which we shall discover our true self and all needs will be met.

It should be obvious that for purpose of prayer

New Testament prayers hold preeminence over all other passages whose nature and purpose are not prayer. If this is to be so in fact as well as in principle, however, these prayers must not be approached like other passages. The Lord's Prayer, for example, can be read as an ordinary part of the New Testament with a view to discerning its message, but it is only when we actually pray this prayer that its meaning as God's word is really disclosed. The same is true of the Old Testament psalms and of the hymns and canticles of the New Testament.

While the prayers hold priority, the remainder of the New Testament can also be used in Christian prayer. This chapter deals primarily with the latter, that is, with New Testament texts which are not formally prayers but which can readily become a word of prayer when properly approached and interpreted.

Amazingly, the Second Vatican Council issued no constitution or other document on prayer. Nor have we ever received an encyclical letter or apostolic constitution on this subject from the popes who have extensively addressed so many other aspects of Christian life and commitment in modern times. Not that they have been altogether silent. Prayer has been frequently treated in multiple contexts, and rare is the church document which does not at least allude to it.

Perhaps this state of things can be credited to the church's realization that prayer is an altogether fundamental aspect of church life which must pervade every other. However, our times seem to call for a synthesis on the subject of Christian prayer. In the early church, prayer drew the special attention of the apostles (Acts 6:4). In our busy, prayer-starved world, it calls for our attention as well.

The Witness of the New Testament

A review of the various works in the New Testament provides a precious, indeed normative, witness to the place of prayer in Christian life. Among these works, Luke-Acts stands preeminent. No other book in the canon shows so much interest in prayer and its relationship to the life of Jesus and of the early Christians. Luke-Acts is consequently our primary source for the New Testament witness concerning prayer.

The New Testament witness is threefold. First, attention to the fact that Jesus and the early Christians prayed, as well as to the theological significance of this fact, shows that prayer is a normal and essential expression of Christian living. Second, Luke-Acts reveals how the early Christians prayed and how their prayer related to the biblical expression of God's word, to the events which God had accomplished in and through Jesus, and to the actual teaching of Jesus. Third, it shows how prayer was related to Christianity's many challenges, problems and social situations.

Prayer in the Life of Jesus and the Early Christians

In view of the church's emphasis on prayer throughout the Christian centuries, it should come as no surprise that the early Christians prayed. However, the extraordinary place occupied by prayer in relation to other expressions of Christian life should give us pause for reflection and self-examination.

At a time when Jesus' followers had just survived the passion, death and resurrection of Jesus and when they were awaiting the very birth of the church, Luke tells us that the apostles retreated to the upper room

(Acts 1:13) and "devoted themselves to constant prayer," together with "some women in their company, Mary the mother of Jesus and his brothers" (Acts 1:14). Reading this account in a world where action frequently displaces prayer, would we not expect the early Christians to have been busy in discussion, developing strategy and reorganizing?

A summary of the nascent church's life after the Pentecost event is particularly significant. In Acts 2:42, Luke lists the four major activities which drew the community's devoted attention and which described the distinguishing characteristics of all truly Christian communities. These activities included apostolic teaching, communal life, the breaking of bread and the prayers. That "the prayers" would have been present in such a list indicates the significant role accorded them in Christian living. That the term "prayers" is modified by the definite article shows that the prayers to which the author refers were not just any prayers but Christian prayers which reflected the Christians' own specific identity and stance before God. Such a prayer is included in Luke 11:2-4, which cites the Lord's Prayer. Taught by Jesus, this prayer enabled Christians to distinguish themselves from the followers of John the Baptist with whom they primitively had been associated (Lk 11:1).

Acts includes many other references to prayer in the early church. Of all of these, however, none brings out the place of prayer in early Christian life so forcefully as 6:4. In a brief account (6:1-7) which introduces the church's apostolic movement from its origins in Jerusalem to its establishment in the Syrian capital of Antioch (6:1-12:25), we find the apostles hard pressed by complaints of discrimination. As a result the twelve recognize that the problem is deeper than it appears. The Jerusalem community's growth and social diversification was calling them away from their primary functions as apostles. Accordingly, they proceeded to expand the group of ministries. Others will see to the equitable distribution of necessities and to the table fellowship. They themselves will concentrate on prayer and the ministry of the word. Associated with the twelve, prayer is thus defined as one of the church's absolutely primary responsibilities. Among the various ministries, it even takes precedence over service at the Christian table. Without prayer and the ministry of the word, all other expressions and forms of Christian life and service are meaningless.

In light of the above reflections, which reveal Luke's in-depth appreciation of prayer, we may better appreciate the prayer context of the annunciation narratives in the Gospel (1:10) as well as the account of the Holy Spirit's descent on Jesus in 3:21-22. The latter took place not during his baptism by John but later while he was at prayer. The voice from heaven reveals Jesus' identity and the depths of his union with God. Jesus' entire mission and journey (4:14-24:53) is thus accounted for in terms of his prayer and the Holy Spirit. As human or Son of Adam (3:38), Jesus prays. As Son of God (3:38), he manifests God's life in human life.

Prayer is especially important when Jesus is confronted by the passion, the ultimate and crowning event of his life, the event which would reveal the full significance of his life, deeds and teaching (Lk 22:41-46). Those who had accompanied Jesus on his journey must pray as he did lest they falter when they too arrive at the journey's climax and passage to God (22:40, 46). Their prayer sprang from a hope made secure by Jesus' own prayer for them (22:31-32). From Jesus' dying words, the Christians also learned how to pray for their enemies (23:34; John 19:17) and to commend themselves to God's hands (23:46). In Acts 7:59-60, the dying Stephen made both prayers his own. Now that Jesus was risen to glory, however, he addressed them directly to the Lord Jesus rather than to the Father. Through the undying prayer of the Lord Jesus, his prayer would reach the Father (see Lk 10:21-22).

Nature, Point of Departure and Method   According to the New Testament, prayer sprang from the personal and communal experience of the early Christians. A major component in their experience was their faith in God the Father, who had granted them new life through and in Jesus Christ their Lord. Concretely, that life had been sparked by the gift of the Holy Spirit and the Gospel word.

In the earliest days, prayer was shaped by the exigencies and implications of Jesus' death-resurrection. Such is the context for Acts 1:14 and the summary of life in the Jerusalem community in Acts 2:42-47.

When Jesus died and entered into glory, he rose to immortal life and the hope of all mankind was fulfilled. By the same token, he also moved out of history and ceased to act as a distinct historical figure with all the limitations of earthly life. Prayer, however, is an activity of mortal human beings along life's journey. It is the activity of those who recognize their creatureliness before God, the creator and source of life, and who turn to God in trusting hope that their deepest aspirations will be fulfilled by him. As risen Lord, Jesus no longer prays in this way. But then, precisely as risen Lord, he also assumed a new mode of presence in the world. He continues to live and act in history through the lives of those who acknowledged his lordship and were transformed by their relationship to him. Christians thus give human, historical expression to the prayer of the risen Lord. Such is the nature of Christian prayer.

The best pattern for Christian prayer was the prayer of Jesus who had shared the Christians' earthly existence and whose prayer had been fulfilled in glory. At a very early date, the Christians thus began to pray according to the prayer of Jesus. However, the resurrection of Jesus had profoundly affected their relationship to God, and they also had to take their new life into account. Jesus' prayer was transformed accordingly. This is reflected in Luke's model of Christian prayer (11:2-4), which is introduced not as Jesus' prayer but as the Lord's Prayer (11:2). During Jesus' historical life, the disciples had observed Jesus at prayer, and he had taught them to pray according to their life and mission as his disciples. As Lord, he continued to inspire and teach them in light of their experience of the passion-resurrection.

In Luke 11:13, the gift of the Holy Spirit summarizes every element of their prayer, namely the hallowing of the Father's name, the coming of his kingdom, the daily gift of their special meal, the forgiveness of sins through their forgiveness of others and preservation from succumbing to the trial (11:2-4).

Later, when Peter and John pray that the Samaritans might receive the Holy Spirit (Acts 8:15), their prayer can consequently be spelled out in terms of the Lord's Prayer (Lk 11:2-4). Gifted with the Spirit, the Samaritans would effectively work for the hallowing of the Father's name and for the other terms of the Lord's Prayer. In Acts 4:31, God's response to the prayer of the

Jerusalem community is a new outpouring of the Holy Spirit, which energizes them for the ministry of the word. Through that ministry, they would work for the kingdom. Jesus' own prayer had been greeted with the gift of the Holy Spirit (Lk 3:21-22). So gifted, he had shared the Father's table fellowship with others and extended his reconciliation to all who accepted it.

Awareness of the Father's gift of new life did not obscure the difficulties of Christian living. From one point of view, every New Testament work represents early Christianity's manifold reaction against a variety of escapist tendencies. This reaction is reflected in the synoptic accounts of Jesus' prayer at the Mount of Olives (Mk 14:32-42; Mt 26:36-46; Lk 22:39-46), accounts which include several elements of the Lord's Prayer. As in Luke 11:1-4, the prayer of Christians is related to that of Jesus himself. Jesus' personal acceptance of the Father's will in the passion (Lk 22:42) provides a model in their own confrontation with the test or trial (Lk 22:40, 46). The envisaged trial (see Lk 11:4) would be their passion and they must respond to it in prayerful acceptance of the Father's will, just as Jesus had accepted his passion.

The Christians prayed according to the prayer of Jesus, but like Jesus their prayer was also according to the scriptures. For all its uniqueness, the prayer of Jesus took up the language of the Jewish and biblical prayer which he came to fulfill. As his followers, the Christians also turned to the Old Testament for the language of prayer. A good example of this can be found in the prayer of the Jerusalem community after the release of Peter and John from prison (Acts 4:24-30). After addressing God as sovereign Lord and creator of all (Acts 4:24; see Gen 1:1-2:4a), they turn to Psalm 2:1-2 and apply these verses to those who had imprisoned them (Acts 4:25-26). Reflecting on Jesus' passion and death, they see their own sufferings as continuous with these (Acts 4:27). Like the conspiracy against Jesus, the persecution which they suffered had been planned by God in Old Testament times and unwittingly fulfilled by their enemies (Acts 4:28). They conclude by asking that God now show himself in the cures, signs and wonders to be worked in the name of Jesus, his holy servant (Acts 4:29-30). The community thus prays as Jesus had prayed, in the recognition that they are to continue the work of God which he had performed during his historical life. Their prayer is God's very own word (Acts 4:29b), and their work is to be in Jesus' name or person (Acts 4:30b).

Concrete Setting in Life As a people of prayer, the early Christians prayed according to the prayer of Jesus and according to the scriptures. We now turn to the concrete historical contexts in which they prayed and to the New Testament's catechesis of prayer.

Is there any moment when Christians are without need? In Luke 18:1-8, the Gospel presents a parable on the necessity of praying always. In the historical and social context of the Lukan communities, this message was especially pertinent. Events were not unfolding according to expectations. Persecution from outside the community, defections from within, the failure of church leadership to serve as Christ served, and the distortion of values had led many to lose heart. They had been praying, but to what effect? God did not appear to be answering their prayer. Were their Gospel hopes groundless? Was their prayer in vain?

Jesus responds with a comparison. If even an unjust judge finally gives in to the persistent pleading of a poor widow for justice, how can anyone think or feel that God who is just will fail to respond to the Christians' prayer for the kingdom? The basic issue is faith. Without faith, no prayer will be uttered, Christians will not acknowledge God's sovereign rule, and the church's active quest and mission for the kingdom will be frustrated. Prayer is not only an expression of faith and hope that the kingdom will indeed be established. It is an effective sign of its actual presence.

This parable is immediately followed by another. In 18:1-8, Jesus had in mind those who were losing heart. In 18:9-14, he addresses those who believe in their own self-righteousness and hold everyone else in contempt. It is not enough to have faith and to be persistent in prayer. One must also pray humbly. The kingdom of God cannot exist without a humble and genuinely self-accepting humanity. As in so many areas, the example of humility comes from unexpected quarters.

In the parable, Jesus compares two men who went to the temple to pray. A Pharisee, whose prayer is proud and self-exalting and who thinks that his material fidelity to religious observances is a sign of his justification, leaves the temple unjustified. A tax collector, whose prayer is humble, who recognizes that he is a sinner and who pleads for divine mercy, leaves the temple justified.

In prayer, it is not the one who prays but the God to whom he or she prays who must be exalted. For this, one must acknowledge humanity's creaturely stance before God the creator and source of life. Such prayer counters the human temptation to want to be like God (Gen 3:5). It corresponds to Jesus' acceptance of all that it means to be human (Phil 2:6-8) and as in the case of Jesus (Phil 2:9-11), it leads to the Christian's exaltation (Lk 18:14). Prayer is thus an extension of baptism's response to the evil which lies at the origins of every other human evil.

The expressions of thanksgiving found at the beginning of Paul's letters help us to discern the various aspects of prayer for men and women engaged in the Christian mission. In every letter except Galatians, these thanksgiving units are found immediately after the introductory address and greeting. The letter to the Philippians provides an excellent example (1:3-11).

Paul's experience with the Philippians had been good. As with every community, there were problems, but the Philippian community had the Christian resources and the integrity to resolve them. There was also need for growth, but the community's history was a solid promise that it would occur.

Describing his prayer, Paul speaks of his giving thanks, rejoicing, pleading (1:3), certitude (1:6), expectations (1:7), personal longing, and an affection which is that of Christ Jesus attitudinally incarnate in him (1:8). He refers to the community's previous history as a continual promotion of the Gospel (1:5), of the Philippians' present sharing in the suffering which the defense of the Gospel entails (1:7), and of their perseverance in the future up to the day of Christ's final manifestation (1:6, 10). Their entire history is the story of how the Gospel seed of Jesus is ripening in them unto a rich harvest (1:11). Faith rooted in God's previous work in them and charity or love shown in their Christian suffering in pursuit of the mission are the basis of Paul's prayer which looks to the future and articulates its hope. Such are the dynamics of Pauline prayer.

162

Our brief review of prayer in the New Testament shows how various authors witness to all aspects of Christian prayer, beginning with its primacy in Christian life. Taken together, these and other statements complement one another in a synthesis on prayer, its nature and wellspring, its development, fundamental expression and method, as well as its concrete historical and social context. This review will guide our steps as we now take up our own use of the New Testament in prayer and some of the modes of interpretation which release its vitality. With the New Testament, Christians join their forebears in speaking and listening to our Father in heaven and his Son who shared our history.

Praying with the New Testament

To pray with the New Testament it does not suffice to know how Christians prayed in New Testament times. One must be touched by the same spark of prayer which quickened their spirit and one must share in those attitudes which were characteristic of early Christianity. It is also imperative to approach and interpret the New Testament in a manner which is appropriate for prayer.

The use of the New Testament in contemporary prayer may take various forms. In the following pages I shall focus on prayerful reading, meditative prayer, and formal prayer, in which the Christian addresses God or Christ our Lord directly.

Prayerful Reading   Prayerful reading of the New Testament may be approached as an activity which has value in itself or as a preparation for meditation or prayer. In either case, the activity is essentially the same.

Not all reading of the New Testament is prayerful. For example, one can read the New Testament in order to discover the origins of Christianity and to have a better understanding of our roots. Perhaps our specific purpose in this is to explore the early formulations of faith or the development of an institution like the Eucharist. Or again, we may be looking for situations in the New Testament which correspond to our own and where the New Testament message can accordingly be adapted to our own life contexts. One could also be in search of the cultural and anthropological understanding which undergirds New Testament writings and releases their meaningfulness, or perhaps it is the forms of literary communication which interest us.

In all the above, the purpose of reading is to gain understanding. Such reading is of definite value. However, it should not be confused with prayerful reading, which approaches the text in a spirit of religious respect and personal openness. An example will help us to appreciate the difference.

In 1 Corinthians 15:1-58, Paul presented an extensive development on the resurrection of Christians and its relationship to that of Christ. We might read the chapter to gain perspective on an important Christian creed (15:3b-5), its relationship to tradition and the Gospel's proclamation (15:1-3a, 6-11), and its implications for the resurrection of Christians (15:12-58). We might explore the unit to discover the source of the creed's vitality as a community develops from its origins. Perhaps it is Paul's assumptions and mode of argumentation which interest us, or how the resurrection could be explained for a people which did not share

Paul's presuppositions concerning the constitution of a human being and the nature of death. In a reading which aims to be prayerful, all of these approaches are distractions. They may fill the time set aside for prayerful reading when someone cannot pray or when someone balks at the challenge of prayer, but they are not prayerful.

There is an even greater danger that we may confuse prayerful reading with an apostolic or pastoral reading of the New Testament. In this case, we focus on the text's meaning for others and on how we would communicate it in the developmental process of evangelization, in catechesis or in homiletics. Prayerful reading, on the other hand, sees the text as addressing the reader. No less than reading for understanding, apostolic and pastoral reading is an escape from prayer. Since the scriptures are God's word and since we are in truth the ministerial agents of that word, we can all too easily deceive ourselves into viewing every reading of the New Testament as prayerful.

A prayerful reading of 1 Corinthians 15 does not focus on what the text can teach us or on how we can use it to reach out to others in Gospel service but on God who speaks to us through our reading of this text. A prayerful reading is an encounter with God who reveals himself to us through the New Testament passage and who calls for our personal response to him.

As an activity, prayerful reading consists primarily in listening. From the point of view of our personal disposition, it consists in openness, acceptance and willingness to be healed, nourished and transformed by God. In prayerful reading we thus stand in a position analogous to men and women being initially evangelized or who are listening to the scriptures in a homiletic context.

To appreciate God's word in our human and Christian context, we must be open to the human author and to his intended readers. In reading 1 Corinthians 15, we stand before Paul as he addresses others and we join the Corinthian community in listening to his word. We also stand in Paul's position and accept to be agents of the Gospel. This calls for two kinds of reading, both of which have distinct value in prayerful reading. In the first case, we see ourselves as addressed by the Gospel and challenged to be consistent in our beliefs and attitudes. In the second, we see ourselves as ministers of the Gospel and appeal for attitudes which are consistent with those of Paul.

As the hearers of God's word spoken by Paul, we must be able to listen. The process can be compared to ordinary human communication, where it becomes essential to attend to the person as well as to what the person is saying. In order to attend to the person, we must approach him or her with respect and openness, aware that we will be transformed by the encounter. We must consequently be willing to undergo transformation, and such willingness requires that we be able to risk venturing in the unknown. These risks are threatening to our resistance to change as well as to our deep-rooted tendency to maintain ourselves in secure positions. However, the reward for taking them is great. As we open ourselves to God's word, we not only grow as Christians, we actually expand our potential for growth. If any encounter with a good person is transforming and creative, how much more creative is an encounter with God, who is the source of all life, including our Christian life?

When we read, for example, that Christ "died for our sins in accordance with the scriptures" (1 Cor 15:3b), God speaks to us of an event, Christ's death, which took place for our benefit as we struggle to emerge from our sinfulness and he states that this fulfills a promise long affirmed in our history as interpreted by the scriptures. If we have a sense of what death means, we cannot but be in awe of such an event. If we recognize our sinfulness, we cannot but respond in gratitude for what was done for us. Aware of our participation in the story of evil and sin, we ask that we be forgiven our rejection of God's gift and our resistance to the story of goodness and virtue. We pray that we may be open to his gift in the future and that we may join in the Gospel story of salvation. In the process we become transformed by Christ's death, and we emerge as a new people on the way of life.

Our prayerful reading thus follows the pattern which characterized the prayer of so many holy men and women throughout the Christian era. Its movement follows the multiple purpose of the Eucharist itself. From the standpoint of prayer, the Eucharist unfolds dynamically as the church's adoration, thanksgiving, reparation and petition, the perfect response to God who creatively reaches out to us in the celebration. In the 19th century, St. Peter Eymard (1811-1868), whom Pope John XXIII canonized as a heroic Christian witness for our time, extensively developed this eucharistic grounding of Christian prayer.

While still viewing ourselves as the people to whom the text is addressed, we may also move from our passive stance as men and women who benefit from Christ's death to an active stance in which we assume

Christ's attitude and join him in offering our lives for the sins of the world. This too is according to the scriptures. Not only do we benefit from Christ's mission, we ourselves take on his mission and extend it through history. It is in this sense that Christian spirituality speaks of a disinterested love which is manifested in a gift of self. Inspired by Christ, our gift is a continuation of his salvific incarnation through history and in the many cultures which contribute to the development of the human community. These notions also formed integral elements of St. Peter Eymard's spirituality.

As men and women who stand with Paul in speaking the word, we see ourselves as communicating God's word. Transformed by the word, we know that we must share it with others. Such a stance also constitutes a prayerful transforming reading. Is this a word which we can personally speak? Our message is not a comfortable one for us. It forces us to confront the false security which we may have assumed *vis-a-vis* our brothers and sisters and society at large. It calls for humility on our part and an attitude which is pure and not self-seeking. As Peter Eymard saw it, humility is the mark of anyone who wishes to pray and live in a manner inspired by the Eucharist.

Recognizing our sinfulness and lack of dedication, a reading of 1 Corinthians 15 in which we stand with Paul challenges our pride and moves us to humility. How else could we say with him, "Last of all he was seen by me, as one born out of the normal course" (I Cor 15:8)? "I am the least of the apostles; in fact, because I persecuted the church of God, I do not even deserve the name. But by God's favor I am what I am" (1 Cor 15:9-10a).

Meditative Prayer   A prayerful reading of the New Testament should normally leave us with a sense of wonder. Like Jesus' father and mother, we have been addressed by God's word (Lk 2:29-32) and we marvel at what has been said (Lk 2:33). We may not have understood the saying which Jesus spoke to us (Lk 2:50), but with Mary we keep everything in our heart (Lk 2:51). Our wonder is also that of Peter after he discovered that Jesus was no longer in the tomb and that everything associated with his death had been left behind (Lk 24:12).

The wonder which prayerful reading has elicited in us is the point of departure for meditative prayer on the New Testament. Without such wonder, meditation becomes mechanical and spiritually empty. Uninspired by the text our efforts are Spiritless.

Like reading, which may or may not be prayerful, meditation is not necessarily prayer. It too can dissolve into study or theological reflection. As St. Augustine defined it, theology is faith in search of understanding. Such study is not only useful but necessary for guiding the church. However, it is not meditative prayer, which searches out the implications of the New Testament for one's life, growth and commitment.

Just as prayerful reading could be compared to the stance of the evangelized in initial or primary evangelization, meditative prayer is akin to the three stages of ongoing evangelization, in which Christians engage in the quest for consistency, the search for a life-synthesis and the integration of ambiguity. Just as prayerful reading could be compared to the hearing of scriptural readings in the liturgy, meditative prayer can be compared to the homily.

169

Prayerful reading was viewed primarily as a listening activity. To the extent that it includes a response, the latter is comparable to that of the psalm response which follows the first reading in the liturgy and the alleluia which precedes the Gospel. For the most part, the response is unarticulated. It surfaces mainly to maintain the flow of communication and to involve the reader in further listening as the text unfolds. It is like the "Amen, brother," the "Amen, sister" and the "Alleluia" of a congregation personally involved in an evangelical service of the word. In prayerful reading, praise, thanksgiving, reparation and petition remain largely at the level of unspoken attitude, open to God and his transforming power, but unrelated to the concrete and specific challenges of the reader.

Meditative prayer with the New Testament starts where prayerful reading ends. Its primary activity is reflection, and it flows into a specific personal response to God's word. Its effectiveness and depth presuppose a measure of catechesis on the New Testament as well as on the challenge of life in our modern world. Someone who has explored Martha's story, for example, and who recognizes the implications of Luke's message in that story for contemporary life and the renewed liturgy will engage in a meditative prayer which articulates God's word precisely as spoken through the Lukan narrative.

The prayerful reading of a New Testament passage is always an interpretation. At least implicitly, the text is seen through the experience of the reader who joins in a new event of divine and human communication. What was implicit must now be made explicit in meditative prayer, and the process of purification and transformation in which the reader has become engaged must be spelled out in terms of each one's life and social context.

Only in this way will it become an effective agent of change and personal sanctification.

A specific example will show how this is realized. The text I have selected is a story. It appears in the Lukan prologue (1:5-2:52) and tells of an angelic appearance to Mary in which she dialogues with Gabriel on the meaning of her life and accepts to bear the life of God's Son for a world in need of divine life (1:26-38). However, she does not yet know what this will require of her as a young Jewish woman immersed in the turbulent life of a Roman client kingdom which is about to undergo revolutionary changes. In particular, she does not know that her life and decision would be the critical factors in preparing not only those changes but a social transformation which would affect the entire world.

Having read the text in a prayerful way, much like a people being initially evangelized, we are open to God's messenger, accept his Gospel and wait to know what it will require of us. Having read the text as a people who hear it in a liturgical context, we know that it calls for a response and commitment which are unique to the present moment and our own social context. As a people who have been catechized, at least in some measure, we know that the story is told as part of a miniature Gospel which summarizes all of Luke and Acts. Mary is a figure or symbol, albeit historical, for the Christians whose story is told in the remainder of Luke's work, and she is consequently a human symbol for the life, vision and mission of the church and all Christians to come, including ourselves. We have also discovered ourselves in the person of Mary, our challenge in her challenge, and we have accepted her response as our response. However, like her, we have little idea what all of this would mean and in particular how as a consequence our lives would contribute to the advent of God's kingdom.

The story begins by situating the event in time. It is the sixth month (1:26a), that is the sixth month of Elizabeth's pregnancy (1:36b). When Elizabeth, and the Old Testament history of Israel which she symbolizes, had come to her old age and when she was thought to be sterile (1:35a), Elizabeth was full of new life. In her, Israel was ready to be quickened by the advent of Mary's Son, Elizabeth's Lord (1:43-44). Contrary to appearances, there was still life in God's relationship to Israel, and that life would appear in the person and prophetic mission of John the Baptist, who would prepare the Lord's way in history. Nothing is impossible with God (1:37).

At this point, our meditation focuses on our own life, on how it so often appears old and sterile and there is little to indicate that it can yet become the bearer of promise. We attend to all that remains unchristian in our existence, to all that has not been transformed by Christ. Of ourselves, we have no grounds to hope that the hidden and not-so-hidden aspects of our personalities can be touched by God's life-giving power. To reach out to Christ, however, we know that we must be alive and ready to prepare his way in us. In Elizabeth's experience, we discover that, contrary to all human expectations, we are in our sixth month, alive with the promise. Hope-filled, we look to the future, ready to greet the fulfillment, Christ our Lord. Nothing is impossible with God.

The story then introduces the messenger, who will reveal the purpose of Elizabeth's unexpected pregnancy. The angel Gabriel was sent from God to a city of Galilee named Nazareth, to a virgin named Mary who was betrothed to a man named Joseph, of the house of David (1:26b). The city, the virgin, her betrothed and his lineage all have to be named. They are unknown, humanly unimportant, and in their lowliness (1:48, 52) have little grounds to warrant an extraordinary role in history. In their very lowliness, however, they could also reveal the Lord's greatness (1:46), might (1:49) and timeless mercy (1:50).

Who among us is really important? In relation to God, who is not lowly? However, we are in our sixth month, full of promise, and the Lord does send his messenger to us. In our lowliness, God offers to fulfill the hopes of the human race. Can we recognize his messenger? The Lord is indeed great, mighty and merciful.

Gabriel's greeting is deeply troubling and mysterious (1:29). "Rejoice," the angel says to Mary, "O highly favored daughter! The Lord is with you. Blessed are you among women" (1:28). Mary has been singled out in Israel for a special mission. In her the covenant, which is summarized in the expression, "The Lord is with you," would be fulfilled, on condition that she accepts to reciprocate and to be with the Lord.

Can God's angel really be speaking to us? We are but a lowly people. How can we be highly favored? How is the Lord with us? How can we be deemed blessed among all who conceive and extend human life to others? There must be some mistake. God's angel must have been sent to someone else. In Mary, however, we have heard the greeting, mysterious as it is, and it remains for us to accept God's offer of covenant that he may be not only with us but with all.

Troubled and wondering at the greeting's meaning, Mary is afraid (1:29-30a). However, the angel continues and calms her fear. "Mary," she is addressed by name, a gesture which summons her unique and non-duplicatable human worth. The purpose of the greeting is about to be unveiled. The mystery transcends all human expectations. Mary has found favor with God. She is to bear a son and give him the name Jesus. No ordinary human being, Mary's Son will be great in dignity. This is already indicated by the fact that his name, and human identity, is God-given. However, he would also be called the Son of the Most High. The Lord will give him the throne of David his father (1:30b-32a) to whom Jesus was related through Joseph (1:26). His role, however, would far transcend the earthly kingdom of his royal forebear. It would fulfill the patriarchal promise in an endless, eternal reign (1:32b-33).

In Mary, we too are troubled, and her fear is our fear. We are to conceive God's very life within ourselves and extend that life to the world. Through us, God's Son would come to rule over the promise held forth in our sixth month and reign forever. The life we are called to bring forth will bring about the kingdom of God. The prospect seems overwhelming, far beyond our human potential. However, we too are called by name. As in the case of Mary, the divine vocative evokes our unique human identity and endows it with divine dignity.

Mary, the virgin (1:26), then asks the inevitable question: "How can this be since I do not know man?" (1:34). The angelic messenger responds that her son would not be born through human sexual intercourse, but through the power of God's creative life-giving Spirit. Human procreation could account for Jesus' humanity. This humanity, however, does not express his full or true identity. Since Jesus was divine, the source of his life could only be divine. The Holy Spirit

174

would consequently come upon Mary and overshadow her. Thus it is that her son Jesus would be called Son of God (1:35).

With Mary, we are well aware of the limits of human life. How can we, through our own human principles for generating life, possibly become the bearers of God's life? In terms of divine life, we all stand virginal before God. Human potential is not the source of divine life. God's Son, however, will come to life in us through the power of the Spirit, a power manifest in Pentecost (Acts 2:1-4), through which God's Son is born in us in order to bring about God's reign through history, in the world, and into eternity.

The new life which Elizabeth and the Old Testament have conceived is Mary's sign that God was ready to fulfill his age-old promise (1:36). She responds with acceptance. She is the servant of the Lord. Let it be done to her as God's messenger says (1:38). The Lord was with her (1:28). She accepted to be with him. The new covenant would be realized.

Mary articulates our response. Recognizing our human potential as a sign that God would fulfill his promise, and open to God's invitation, we place ourselves in God's service for the kingdom. The implications of that service are indicated in the Gospel's narrative of the life and mission of Jesus, the son of Adam and the Son of God, the human being who is divine (3:38), and who insists that the way of God in history is the fully human way (4:1-13).

In our meditative prayer, we have discovered that Mary's most unique prerogative lies in the way she provides the true pattern for every Christian's life and mission. Nothing is impossible with God.

Formal Prayer In our prayerful reading of a New Testament passage, we listened to God's human word and that word filled us with wonder. In our meditative prayer, we reflected on God's word, saw its implications, came to grips with our fear and articulated our response to God's invitation. Still filled with wonder, we are now left with a feeling of joyful eagerness to plunge into life's Christian challenge. Before we do so, however, we have a need to speak to God. He spoke to us, and we must answer. Just as listening and reflection were the characteristic activities of prayerful reading and meditative prayer, speaking is that of formal prayer.

Are we not naive, however, in thinking that we can speak to God? Are we not deceived in believing that we are actually doing so? From the point of view of communication, is not such speech illusory? When we speak to God, are we not rather speaking to ourselves?

In a sense, we are speaking to ourselves, but to ourselves in our Christian identity as human expressions of God's presence in the world. The Christian may find God in the universe and in the neighbor. The greatest challenge, however, is to be able to discover the divine presence in our deepest and truest self, in which all falsehood is unmasked. There is much falseness in us, of course, but the very process of prayer gradually dispels all that is not true. Through prayer, God's image in us becomes increasingly sharper as we come to participate more and more in the life of one who is our Father as well as the Father of Jesus the Lord.

Do we need human words to speak to God in this way? At the beginning of prayer, we do usually need words, limited as they are, and we spontaneously turn to them. To speak is human, and it is in speech that we normally grasp our relationship to God and clarify our needs. We may even discover our needs when we try to articulate them. As we pray, however, we frequently pass the point where words are adequate and we begin to communicate in silence. Such silence is that of deep communication and not of isolation, distance and refusal to communicate. Were we to begin our prayer with silence, it might too easily remain vague and superficial. When silence follows a spoken address to God, however, it comes as an experiential exigency and reflects our attunement with the mystery of God's life which is vibrant within us. Such prayer is the prayer of contemplation.

Formal prayer can be compared to the prayer of the faithful in the eucharistic liturgy. Once we have listened to the word and reflected on it as in the homily, we voice our needs to the Lord and ask that he hear our prayer. The quality of such prayer depends on the maturity which we have reached in our personal evangelization and catechesis. One who has heard the Gospel and integrated it in life knows which needs are truly significant. The prayer which flows from this faith knowledge, in which the law of love and justice is written in the heart, is a selfless prayer which seeks God's reign in all things. Every other need is secondary and subordinate to this most Christian of needs.

As in the liturgical prayer of the faithful, formal prayer moves away from the prayerful reading of scripture and its meditative reflection. Presupposed, these activities orient the content of prayer and provide its religious inspiration. The prayer itself, however, is spoken in words which well up from our own experience and historical situation and not in the words of the biblical author, except in the measure that these are appropriate to express our personal stance before God in the present moment.

Formal prayer is thus a Christian response to God's historical word, but insofar as it has broken into our consciousness as a living and abiding word. That word is the Gospel which has been preached to us but which has also become reincarnate in us. So internalized, it is like a seed, not a corruptible seed but an incorruptible one, which has been planted in us (1 Pt 1:22-25). True to its nature, the biblical word of God has become a new expression of revelation, and our prayer responds to that revelation in faith, love and hope.

An example from the book of Acts will prove useful. In Acts 8:26-40, we read of an encounter between Philip and an Ethiopian on the Gaza road.

In our prayerful reading, we may have identified with the Ethiopian who has been reading the text of Isaiah 53:7-8 and who was trying to understand its message concerning a sheep led to the slaughter and deprived of his life on earth. The sheep is obviously a metaphorical expression for a human being. As Christians, we already surmise that the sheep is Jesus. However, we do not grasp, at least not fully, what his slaughter or passion meant or implied. We may also have identified with Philip, who opened the scriptures for the Ethiopian, showed him how the slaughter was actually the Good News of Jesus and responded affirmatively to the Ethiopian's request for baptism. We may also have noted how the story parallels that of the two disciples of Emmaus, except that the Emmaus event climaxed not in baptism but in the breaking of the bread (Lk 24:13-35).

In our meditative prayer, we reflected on the close similarity between our own situation and that of Philip and the Ethiopian. We too grope to understand the slaughter of human beings and of Jesus' own followers in our world. The biblical text, like the passage from Isaiah, is opaque for us until we discover that the death of those who die with Christ is meaningful and truly good news. The very nature of Christian baptism claims as much. We also come to grips with our responsibility to open the scriptures for others in a mutual exchange which leads to faith understanding and commitment. We know that we must explain the scriptures in such a way that others seek baptism or renew their baptism's pledge to live as Jesus lived and to die with him for the sake of others. What does this require of us? Each one answers according to his or her uniqueness, responsibilities and generosity.

In our formal prayer, we may pray in words such as the following: Lord, we are on a journey, emerging from our past, struggling not to cling to it, and moving along a way which was first traced by Jesus your Son. Join us on that journey. May it be for us a journey of discovery. Help us to understand what the journey requires. Send your messengers to us to unveil the meaning of the scriptures concerning Jesus' Good News for us. May we have the openness to welcome your messengers. Send us as your messengers to others. We are ready to hear your word and ready to speak it. Without you, however, we can do neither. Thank you for your promise of guidance and assistance. We know that the promise will continue to be fulfilled. We praise you with our words. May we do so with our lives.

Inspired by the scripture text, formal prayer remains close to the biblical word even as it brings the scriptures to life in a new world. The scriptures thus provide a guide for both its content and expression.

179

Even so, however, it retains the risk of wandering away from the Christian heritage as lived in the church community. To obviate this danger, the New Testament provides us with a normative prayer whose movement outlines that of all genuinely Christian prayer and whose form of address and petitions constitutes a generic expression of all Christian prayer. That prayer is the Lord's Prayer, found in Matthew 6:9-13 and Luke 11:2-4.

The difference between the two synoptic versions of the Lord's Prayer is not a problem when we view the prayer as a model prayer rather than as a specific formula. From the standpoint of the New Testament, the Lord's Prayer indicates not so much what Christians say in prayer but how a Christian prays. Its wording was thus considered quite flexible from its very origins.

As a normative statement of the movement of Christian prayer, the Lord's Prayer begins by addressing God directly, "Father" or "Our Father in heaven." It then asks that the vision of Jesus and his followers, including ourselves, be realized. That vision includes the hallowing of the Father's name, the coming of his kingdom, and as Matthew adds the accomplishment of his will on earth as it is in heaven. The realization of this vision, however, is a matter of concern for those who live on earth and who join in a common responsibility to bring it about. The prayer thus continues, takes up the essential means for realizing the vision, and asks for the Christian realities and attitudes required in the mission as it moves through history.

Formal prayer follows the same movement by first articulating the relationship between the one who prays and God who is addressed. In so doing, it expresses our attentiveness and readiness to have our prayer fulfilled and it attunes us to God's own faithful attentiveness and unswerving readiness to fulfill our prayer. Second, every prayerful need, whatever it may be, is situated in the context of the Gospel vision which defines the entire purpose of Christian life. We thus never depart from the fundamental sense of God and life which came to us through evangelization. Third, every prayerful need is also seen in terms of the mission which flows from our Christian identity. Every specific need is seen as some aspect of what enters in the unfolding of this mission.

As a normative statement of the expression of Christian prayer, the Lord's Prayer invokes God as Father and situates every other title or form of address in the context of his life-giving relationship to us. By the same token, we view ourselves as men and women who draw their life from him. If God is our Father, we are his sons and daughters. The Lord to whom we pray is thus a transcendent Father who is not subject to us. As his sons and daughters, on the other hand, we are more than subjects but children for whom the life already given is a divine pledge of ongoing life for the future. All that we pray for is consequently an expression of the life which God shares with us.

God's name is a symbolic term which refers to his personal being as communicated to human beings. We dare not assign him a specific name as we do for ourselves. Rather, we recognize that he has a name, that it is fully known only to himself, but that it is also partially and progressively disclosed to those who know him. By giving God a name, we would limit him, align him with ourselves, reduce him to creaturely status and by the same token refuse to acknowledge his transcendence. The name would become a verbal idol.

God's name must be hallowed. With this petition,

181

we ask that the Father's personal being be acknowledged and manifested in the life of every human being. Such is the first expression of the Christian vision. It summarizes the very purpose of human life on earth and accepts that we contribute actively to the fulfillment of that purpose.

The kingdom and the will of the Father represent two alternate ways of referring to the hallowing of the name but with different emphases. The kingdom metaphor is drawn from earthly political life and emphasizes the social aspect of the Father's relationship to his sons and daughters. If God reigns, his rule must be reflected in the roles, attitudes and relationships which obtain among subjects who draw life from him. The will articulates the effectiveness of his self-manifestation through the name and of his relationship to human society as sovereign Lord.

No formal prayer is truly Christian unless it refers at least implicitly to these various ways of expressing the Christian vision. The hallowing of the name, the coming of the kingdom and the doing of God's will undergird and motivate every statement made in formal prayer.

After addressing God as Father, we pray for humanity's acceptance of the Father's self-disclosure, for submission to his reign, and for attunement to his will. Such is the vision toward which we tend. It coincides with the very purpose of creation. In the second set of petitions, we pray for a truly Christian meal, for the forgiveness of sins, and for assistance in meeting our history's ultimate temptation or test. Such are the components of life in the Christian mission. They coincide with the very purpose of redemption or salvation.

The bread which characterizes Christian life is a bread broken and shared, an event in which Christ offers himself for the life of the world. In our Christian bread or meal, we too offer ourselves for others and become the sacramental expression of Christ's self-offering. This bread for which we pray constitutes a symbolic expression of the church community's entire effort to reach out to others with the transforming gift of Christ's presence. Of ourselves, this gesture is impossible. It is God's work of salvation through Christ, and so we must pray for it. It enables us to weigh the value of all our needs as Christ's agents of salvation.

Our entire prayer presupposes that creation and Christian life are developmental processes in which we tend toward our divinely intended fulfillment. The process, however, is not untroubled. Evil and sin are earthly realities which interfere with it and which we cannot ignore. In the Lord's Prayer, we thus ask the Father for the forgiveness of our sins. Just as we progressively find life by giving it for others, forgiveness is granted through our forgiveness of others. Every other expression of prayer must be equally altruistic.

Thrust into a history which moves toward its climactic consummation in death and fullness of life, for the individual as well as for history itself, we end our prayer with a petition for help as we confront that supreme moment, our final test. Every temptation is but a pale reflection of that test. Our prayer that we not succumb to the ultimate temptation (see Lk 22:39, 46) is fulfilled when we join Jesus in turning to the Father with total submission: "Father, if it is your will, take this cup from me; yet not my will but yours be done" (Lk 22:42).

We conclude this unit on praying with the New Testament with a brief summary.

First, we explored the process of prayerful reading, in which the primary activity consists in listening. In those pages, prayerful reading was distinguished from other forms of reading the New Testament, and we saw how prayerful reading can assume at least two forms, one in which we join the addressees and listen to the author's word to us, and one in which we join the author as men and women called to communicate God's word to others.

Exploring meditative prayer, we saw how this form of prayer consists basically in reflection, and we distinguished this activity from other forms of reflection. In those pages, we examined how meditative prayer can view the Gospel stories as expressions of our own concrete life story.

In the section on formal prayer, we saw how such prayer consists primarily in speech or direct communication, an activity which normally leads to our silent response to God. We also showed how formal prayer moves away from the text which inspired it and how the quality of our personal prayer can be measured by the movement and content of the Lord's Prayer.

Bibliographical Note

Since prayer is a major theme in the New Testament, it comes as no surprise that many have written about it. Most of the modern writing deals with one or more aspects of what I have termed the witness of the New Testament. This tendency contrasts with the earlier periods of Christianity, when writings explored the New Testament witness not so much for its own sake but to draw out its implications for Christian life and practice.

The primary focus of much of this writing has been the Lord's Prayer. Rightly so. Tertullian, one of the early Fathers of the church from North Africa, called the Lord's Prayer a "resume of the entire Gospel." The statement appears in Chapter I of his essay "On Prayer" (circa 192), a work which interprets the various clauses of the Lord's Prayer (Chapters II-IX) and uses these as a springboard for discussing many theoretical and practical issues concerning prayer (Chapters X-XXIX; see *Ante-Nicene Fathers*, Grand Rapids: Wm. B. Eerdmans, 1973; Vol. III, pp. 681-691).

In the 13th century, Thomas Aquinas devoted a special article to the Lord's Prayer in his *Summa* of theology (IIa IIae, q. 83, a. 9). His first major statement is that the Lord's Prayer is absolutely perfect. Following Augustine (Letter 130), he affirms that when we pray the Lord's Prayer as it should be prayed, we are unable to find anything further to say. The Lord's Prayer adequately interprets all our legitimate needs before God and presents these in their appropriate order. First, it addresses the goal of Christian life; second, it asks for the means to reach that goal. Aquinas' analysis exerted a profound influence on this chapter, which distinguished the vision, Aquinas' goal or *finis*, found in the first set of petitions, from the mission, Aquinas' means to reach the goal, found in the second set of petitions. Inspired by Aquinas, we also saw the Lord's Prayer as doubly normative; first, from the point of view of movement, Aquinas' order, and second, from that of expression, Aquinas' verbal interpretation of needs.

St. Teresa of Avila, a 16th-century Spanish writer who devoted most of her energies to the renewal of important areas of Christian life, left us *The Way of Perfection*, a truly classic work of enormous influence.

Her own title for this work, however, was not *The Way of Perfection*, but the *Paternoster* or Lord's Prayer, to which she devoted the last 16 chapters of her work (Chapters 27-42). "I am astounded," Teresa wrote, "when I consider that in its few words are enshrined all contemplation and perfection, so that if we study it no other book seems necessary" (Chapter 37). Teresa's appreciation of the Lord's Prayer stands in solid continuity with Christian tradition as illustrated by the judgment of Tertullian, Augustine and Thomas Aquinas. Her work is conveniently available in *Image Books* (Garden City: Doubleday, 1964).

Modern biblical scholarship shares the appreciation of past centuries for the Lord's Prayer, and several major scholars have analyzed the prayer and explored its implications from various points of view.

Among the many works produced, that of Joachim Jeremias, *The Lord's Prayer*, number 8 in the Biblical Series of Facet Books (Philadelphia: Fortress, 1964), is noteworthy for its attention to the prayer's context in the historical life of Jesus. A similar preoccupation can be found in Philip B. Harner's more recent work, *Understanding the Lord's Prayer* (Philadelphia: Fortress, 1975) and in Heinz Schurmann's *Praying with Christ* (New York: Herder and Herder, 1964). Schurmann, however, also studied the prayer in light of the remainder of Jesus' teaching in the Gospels.

Raymond E. Brown, on the other hand, was concerned not so much with the prayer's interpretation in terms of the historical life of Jesus as with its development and understanding in early Christian tradition. As his title indicates, "The Pater Noster as an Eschatological Prayer" (see his *New Testament Essays*,

Garden City: Doubleday, *Image Books*, 1968, pp. 275-320), Brown focuses on the prayer's relationship to eschatology in New Testament times. My own article, "Give Us Each Day Our Daily Bread" (see *Bread from Heaven*, ed. by Paul J. Bernier, New York: Paulist, 1977, pp. 19-33), shares Brown's concern with tradition. Addressing the petition for bread as found in the Lukan version, I emphasized the prayer's relationship to the origins of the eucharistic liturgy.

More recently, I explored the Lukan expression of the Lord's Prayer as part of the Gospel's message to Luke's addressees (*Luke* in *New Testament Message*, Wilmington: Michael Glazier, Inc., 1980, Vol. 5). This commentary interprets the prayer's contribution to Luke's pastoral theology and shows how its petitions have been taken up and developed by many other passages in the Gospel.

Since Paul refers so frequently to prayer, commentaries on his letters cannot but deal with the subject. In these works, however, prayer is treated quite briefly. The same is true of the various efforts to elaborate a synthesis of Paul's theology. David M. Stanley filled this relative vacuum in *Boasting in the Lord* (New York: Paulist, 1973), a sensitive and comprehensive study of the phenomenon of prayer as it appears in the Pauline letters. After showing how Paul's prayer springs from his experience of the risen Christ on the road to Damascus, Stanley explores a number of major experiences which are related to Paul's view of prayer. He then studies the prayers contained in the Pauline letters, Paul's observations on prayer, the shape of his prayer, and the relationship between Pauline prayers and Pauline theology.

While Schurmann's work was primarily concerned with understanding the Lord's Prayer in the context of Jesus' other teaching, it also addressed the pastoral issue of how this prayer serves the life of the church today. It thus provides a bridge to this chapter's main subject, praying with the New Testament. His interest in the experiences and attitudes required of one who wishes to pray the Lord's Prayer also contributed the initial scholarly inspiration for my *Trumpets of Beaten Metal, Biblical Prayer in Post-Biblical Times* (Collegeville: Liturgical Press, 1974). In this short book, I dealt with some of the basic issues of interpretation, but I focused especially on the experience of life, the experience of God and the attitudes of historical solidarity, community consciousness and openness to the future which are presupposed by biblical prayer and which we must share in order to pray with the New Testament.

A series of biblical booklets entitled *Read and Pray* (Chicago: Franciscan Herald), which was designed and edited by Robert J. Karris, suggested this chapter's distinction between the use of the New Testament in meditative prayer and in formal prayer. These booklets, to which Philip Van Linden, Donald Senior, Robert J. Karris, Pheme Perkins and I contributed the Gospels of St. Mark, St. Matthew, St. Luke, St. John, and the Acts of the Apostles, respectively, present a brief exegetical comment, a reflection and a brief prayer for each of 90 consecutive sections of a Gospel or Acts. They thus provide a three-month program of daily prayer for Christians busily engaged in a nervous world whose preoccupations militate against regular prayer. In relation to Karris' format, this chapter's development on prayerful reading should be inserted between the exegetical comment and the reflection included for each scriptural unit.

In his *Biblical Meditations for Lent* (1979), *Easter Season* (1980) and *Advent* (1980), all from Paulist Press, Carroll Stuhlmueller provides excellent models for praying meditatively with the scriptures. Since his brief meditations are based on the text used in the daily and Sunday lectionaries, his books help us to relate personal prayer to liturgical prayer, and they are bound to nourish the spirit of the homilist.

My treatment of the New Testament in prayer began by saying that prayer is a human being's spontaneous response to God. At its conclusion, my prayer is that those who have followed its development can better appreciate how that spontaneous response can coincide with the New Testament, Christianity's classic and normative response to God. Nothing is impossible with God!